Stories
of Karol

Stories of Karol

The Unknown Life of John Paul II

Gian Franco Svidercoschi

Translated by Peter Heinegg

Liguori/Triumph
LIGUORI, MISSOURI

Imprimi Potest:
Richard Thibodeau, C.Ss.R.
Provincial, Denver Province
The Redemptorists

Published by Liguori/Triumph
An imprint of Liguori Publications
Liguori, Missouri
www.liguori.org

Presently published as *Storia di Karol* in 2001 by Ancora, Milano.

Library of Congress Cataloging-in-Publication Data

Svidercoschi, Gian Franco.
   [Storia di Karol. English]
   Stories of Karol : the unknown life of John Paul II / Gian Franco Svidercoschi ; translated by Peter Heinegg.
      p. cm.
   ISBN 0-7648-0924-5
   1. John Paul II, Pope, 1920– 2. Popes—Biography. I. Title.

BX1378.5 .S8813 2003
282'.092—dc21
[B]   2002029863

Scripture quotations, except where noted, are taken from the *New Revised Standard Version Bible*, copyright 1989 by the Division of Christian Education of the National Council of the Churches of Christ in the U.S.A. Used by permission. All rights reserved.

Liguori Publications, a nonprofit corporation, is an apostolate of the Redemptorists. To learn more about the Redemptorist Congregation, visit *Redemptorists.com*.

Printed in the United States of America
09 08 07 06 05   5 4 3 2

CONTENTS

PREFACE

It might seem senseless to present the story of Karol Wojtyla only to stop at his election as pope—particularly now that his pontificate is entering, so to speak, its sunset phase. In view of that, is this now not the time then, after twenty-two intense years of universal ministry, when all the information is available to attempt, if not a final balance sheet of his work, at least a fairly complete portrait of John Paul II?

The decision to tell only this part of his life, the *Story of Karol*, first over Italy's Radio Due program, *Alle 8 della sera* ("At Eight P.M."), and now in a book, derives from a very specific purpose. It is driven by the conviction that there is no way to understand the figure of Pope Wojtyla, the first Slavic pope, unless one goes back to his origins, to the roots of his vocation, and to the different experiences and situations through which he lived.

Above all, of course, there is his family—and then the religious, cultural, and social climate of Poland in the 1930s. After that fact comes World War II, which runs all the way through the first phase of Karol's life, as if it aimed at "accompanying" and marking that life, and not just symbolically. Finally, there is his priestly ministry, his pastoral and intellectual efforts, his episcopacy and participation in the Second Vatican Council.

Additionally, it does not seem possible to grasp the complex meaning of this pontificate—anchored as it is in the defense of the human person, of human dignity and human rights—unless we start out from the dramatic awareness that Karol Wojtyla has had of both Nazism and Communism. His personal story is closely interwoven with—and indelibly stamped by—the story of the two kinds of totalitarianism that, though from different directions and in different forms, have both launched an absolutely unprecedented attempt to destroy the reality of humankind.

In a sense, one could say that Karol Wojtyla sums up in himself, in his person, in his life, the collective destiny of twentieth-century humanity. First, he had direct experience of the two totalitarian cataclysms; second, as a witness, he has borne on the pontifical chair the living and cautionary memory of those tragic pages of history, but also the many hopes, and especially the new hopes, that have burst forth from that same twentieth century.

Thus, once we have traveled back over the human and spiritual itinerary of Karol Wojtyla, it will be easier to realize how all the trials he underwent, how all the experiences he had in his youth, and how his time as a priest and bishop helped to prepare him for the responsibility of the papacy at this specific moment in history and at this specific time in the life of the Church. It comes as no surprise to find a close continuity between the "before" and the "after," not only in his teachings and in his initiatives, but even in his language.

The most significant gestures that he made during the Jubilee Year of 2000—such as his visit to the Western Wall in Jerusalem, his begging of forgiveness for the sins committed by Christians throughout the ages against divine and human truth, his commemoration of the martyrs, especially the thousands of unknown martyrs who have marked this century of totalitarianism with their blood, or his encounter with millions of young people at Tor Vergata—these gestures, every one of them, are the culmination of a path first entered on many years ago in Wadowice and in Cracow.

And now, in seeking to recapitulate, in a sense, all of these factors, we might speak of a pope who has been a "ferryman." In the same fashion as Cardinal Wyszynski had anticipated the Vatican II conclave, here is a pope who, living in an age of transition, has served as a guide and companion in the passage from one millennium to another.

He has accompanied the Church from the crisis of the postconciliar period to a new stage of evangelization, to a new presence in history, with a universal impact never known before. And if there have also been calls to order, intransigent positions, and even abrupt endings, these have to be compared with the numerous "turnabouts" that this pope has accomplished (or at least recommended) even though all the parts of the Church have not always followed his path.

He has accompanied the human race from the collapse of ideologies, of false political and economic messianic faiths (and not just of the Marxist variety), to a fresh awareness of its unity, its common destiny, for which peace and justice and solidarity will never emerge except from respect for the rights of persons and peoples, beginning with the right to life.

But, above all, John Paul II has accompanied contemporary men and women in the difficult ascent out of the abyss into which they had plunged, convinced as they were that they held in their hands absolute power, and up into a new search for significance, for the meaning of existence, to a new consciousness of their own moral actions. He has led them, when all is said and done, to feel a yearning for a God who may be distant, but who has never been completely forgotten.

Chapter One

BORN IN FREEDOM

I

t was May 18, 1920. Back from his military campaign in Ukraine, Marshall Jozef Pilsudski was given a triumphant reception in Warsaw.

After more than a century of slavery, Poland had just barely won back its freedom. The head of the new republic had tried to recover the old eastern borders. He hadn't completely realized his objectives, but he had beaten the Red Army and taken Kiev.

Pilsudski arrived on a special train that was draped in flowers; and he was driven through the streets of the capital between two walls of a wildly cheering throng. A Mass of victory was celebrated in the church of St. Alexander, and a solemn *Te Deum* was sung.

At that very time in Wadowice (also spelled Katowice)— and no doubt in many other Polish cities—a baby was being born. This one saw the light of day in the apartment of the Wojtylas, one side of which looked out on the parish church.

As she was going through labor—it was customary back then to give birth at home—his mother, Emilia, upon hearing the hymns from the novena being held in the church, asked the midwife to open the windows so she could hear the singing.

She then gave birth to Karol Jozef—named Karol after his

father, and Jozef after the emperor Franz Joseph of Austria-Hungary in whose army Wojtyla Senior had fought. The symbolism, though wholly accidental, could not possibly have been more Polish.

From time immemorial, Poland had been deeply stamped by religious tradition: on the eve of Easter in 966, Catholic Poland and the Polish nation had been born together.

The baptism of Duke Mieszko, the founder of the nation, had been prompted by the influence of his Catholic wife, the Czech Princess Dubrawksa. But it is also very likely that there were geopolitical considerations at work as well. With good reason, Mieszko, upon embracing Christianity, had chosen the longer "route": instead of going to Byzantium, he had turned to Rome, to the pope, who would be a much more powerful, authoritative, and powerful protector.

And yet, by bringing Poland into the circuit of Roman Christianity and the Latin West, Mieszko had inadvertently made a fateful decision; he had made Poland a crossroads, a bridge, between two civilizations, between Slavic and western European culture. In this way, even after the schisms that tore Christianity apart, a permanent Catholic presence was installed between the two political and religious blocs: on the one side, the Orthodox world, upheld at first by the tsars, then by the predominant Marxist ideology; and on the other, the German world, mostly imbued with Protestantism.

It has been that way for a thousand years. It was that way in Poland in the 1920s, with the Christian faith firmly rooted in the life and customs of the people. And it was that way in Wadowice in the house across the street from the parish church, with the sound of the bells ringing out the times of the everyday routine. And there was a sundial with a Latin inscription that forced you to think continuously of the things of the spirit: "Time flies," it said, "and eternity awaits."

The city of Wadowice was founded in the thirteenth century along the Skawa River, at the foot of the Beskid Mountains, some forty miles from Cracow. In the center, the Rynek, or marketplace, was framed by the most important buildings: the town hall, the parish church of St. Mary, with its onion dome, and the elementary school. On Thursdays there was a very lively scene when the Rynek filled up the benches with the townsfolk displaying their produce.

There was nothing all that different about Wadowice, then, from the other small towns in the Polish provinces; but Wadowice had three distinctive features. First and above all, there was its intense cultural and social life. It had four high schools, numerous artistic associations, three public libraries, a theater group, and a sports club. Beyond that, Wadowice was the seat for the regional court.

Second, there was at the time a flourishing Jewish community, which made up about one-third of the town's eighteen thousand inhabitants. And, unlike other places in Poland where a certain anti-Semitism still survived the legacy of ancient prejudices, though these were economic and social rather than racial ones, in Wadowice the majority of the Jews were integrated into the life of the town. Instead of conflict there were relations of friendship and respect. Poland had a tradition of ongoing tolerance and hospitality, so much so that during the Reformation it earned the title of the "state without bonfires" (that is, a place where the burning of heretics at the stake was not common).

The third peculiar feature of Wadowice was the barracks lodging the Twelfth Infantry Regiment, famous because its men had participated in the war against the Bolsheviks.

The Wojtylas lived in a modest but respectable apartment at 2 Koscielna Street. The building belonged to a Jew, Mr. Balamuth, who also had a business in the marketplace, selling bicycles and motorcycles. From the courtyard one made one's way up an iron staircase. On the second floor there was a gallery and the entrance, with a little majolica holy water font, then the kitchen, the bedroom, and the living room. There were lots of books, and on the walls hung photos and holy pictures.

Emilia, the lady of the house, kept it all in order. She was a tiny woman with a beauty all her own, and deep black eyes that were at once vivacious and ironic. Although her health was delicate, she had gone back to her old job of embroidering to bolster the family income. Edmund, the elder boy, was about to move to Cracow to study medicine. Thus, there would be more room in the house now that Karol was born; but there would also be a need for more money.

Karol Wojtyla, Sr., was a gentleman of the old school, highly cultured, a passionate lover of history. Austere and severe in appearance, he had a kind and courteous manner. Both his hair and moustache were tinged with gray. In his youth he had been a tailor; then he became a career bureaucrat in the administration of first the Austro-Hungarian, and now the Polish, army. Everyone called him "Captain."

Karol grew up in this serene and peaceful setting, full of piety and patriotism. His was the first generation to be born and raised in freedom, after Poland had been subjugated, oppressed, and violated in its fundamental rights as a nation for one hundred twenty years.

From 1772 to 1795, in three successive partitions, the great powers of the time—Russia, Prussia, and Austria—had erased the country from the map of Europe. The various attempts made to throw off the foreign yoke had come to nothing. Kosciusko's uprising had proved futile. The creation of an autonomous grand duchy under Napoleon had proved futile. The revolt of 1830 against Tsar Nicholas I had also proved futile, as had the one in 1863, likewise put down by the Russian army, with thousands of Polish patriots winding up in Siberian prisons, most of them never to return.

The West had always stood by idly watching, inert and indifferent. "Order reigns in Warsaw." That was how the French foreign minister, Sebastiani, had reported the news to Parliament in a highly realistic but richly cynical tone.

The new century had barely begun when the First World

War broke out. Austria and Germany emerged from it defeated, while Russia was shaken by the October Revolution. Europe had felt the need for peace and had tried to solve the thorniest problems that were still on the table. Finally, in 1919, the Treaty of Versailles had recognized Poland's independence, restoring its western boundaries more or less to their original location.

On the eastern side, the Soviet threat was as strong as ever; but the Poles clung tenaciously to their freedom, which had been recovered with such toil. They were not about to give it up. When, in August of 1920, Lenin launched the cavalry of General Semyon Budenny against Poland, planning to invade Europe after that. Pilsudski and his divisions, incredibly, routed the Red Army. His victory is still remembered today as the "miracle of the Vistula."

The years passed and Karol started school. In the first grade, sitting on the same bench, he found a little boy as skinny as he was and with the same short hair: Jerzy Kluger, the son of a well-known lawyer, who was also a leader of the local Jewish community. They immediately took a liking to each other. Along with their other companions, such as the Piotrowski twins, they went to play soccer; in the summer they splashed in the Skawa River, in the winter they skated and played hockey. The sticks they had were very crude, but the boys had fun anyway.

Then that brutal day arrived: Karol came home from school, and a woman neighbor came out to hug him and murmur, "Your mama has gone to heaven." He looked at her more in surprise than pain, as if she were talking about somebody else's mother. Lately, he had seen little of her; she was ill. But he didn't believe the news. He was barely nine years old. Only much later would he come to feel her absence and begin to talk about her once more.

From that time on, the "Captain," who had already retired, devoted himself completely to his son. They went out to dinner in a little restaurant; but otherwise he took care of everything: preparing meals, washing the dishes, cleaning up. He even managed to cut out a suit for Karol from his old uniform.

He was father and mother to his son; he was always close by. He helped him with his studies. He taught him to read and to pray, to contemplate the mystery of God; but this was far removed from any conformism or churchiness. He did what he could so that his son, later on when he was on his own, would develop a faith that was grownup and full of conviction.

Father and son read the Bible together and recited the rosary. But they also played soccer in the living room with a ball made of rags. When Jerzy Kluger came to do his homework with his friend, the "Captain" would pull out an illustrated history book and talk about Poland's heroic days. Or he would read a poem, like that lovely, enchanting one by Cyprian Norwid entitled "Chopin's Piano." It describes how the uprising of 1863 was stifled in blood, and the dream of Polish independence had once again sunk out of sight. For this reason, the women of Warsaw had decided to dress in mourning. Norwid saw in Chopin the symbol not just of the highest artistic perfection, but also of the path that his homeland should take to regenerate itself and win back its freedom.

> Look!—from one alley to another
> The horses from the Caucasus burst in
> Like swallows before the storm,
> Shooting past the regiments,
> By the hundreds—the hundreds—
> A building burnt, then extinguished,
> Then gone up in flames again—and see
>   —against the wall
> I see the foreheads of the widows in mourning
> Thrust by rifle butts.

The two children listened gaping, their eyes opened wide with emotion. They knew the poet was talking about something that had really happened.

In Warsaw, in November 1863, there had been an assassination attempt on General Friedrich W. R. Berg, the tsarist governor. The palace from which the bombs had been thrown was given over to the soldiers from the Lithuanian Guards to pillage. They chased out the residents, one of whom was Chopin's sister, and threw out of the windows everything in the apartments, including the great musician's piano.

> And, although blinded by the smoke
> once more I see them carry along the colonnade
> Like a coffin shouldered high
> Your piano—that falls—and falls!

Karol was an altar boy. One day in church while he was serving Mass, his friend Jerzy suddenly walked in. A woman looked at him in astonishment and said something to him. He stood there unmoving, frozen in place. Finally, he told his friend Karol that he had come to give him the good news: they had both passed the entrance exam and so next year they would be going to the lyceum where the "big boys" went.

"But what did that lady want?" Karol asked. To which Jerzy replied: "She was surprised to see a Jew in church, and especially the son of the leader of the Jewish community."

Karol broke out into a loud laugh, "But why? Didn't they tell us that we are all God's children?"

Chapter Two

THE BOYS OF WADOWICE

K arol was familiar with the boys' high school or *"gym-nasium"* as it was called. The first time he walked past it on Mickiewicz Street, he had stood in utter fascination at the stark, imposing appearance of the building. Even more, the Latin inscription on the facade elicited a feeling in him that the words held some mysterious meaning. He had often tried to break it down into syllables: *"Et ma-ni-bus pu-ris su-mi-te fon-tis a-quam"* ("And take water from the fountain with pure hands").

But on that day, the first day of class, when he arrived in front of the building, he had a panic attack. To steel himself, he gripped his father's hand. He looked around, searching for his grammar school buddies. Jerzy Kluger was there, and so were the Piotrowski twins, always cheery; they could see the humorous side of everything. But that morning, like him, like Jerzy, they were terrified at the mere thought of having to cross the threshold of the institute.

Those years in the *gymnasium*, from 1930 to 1938, were truly a unique phase in Karol's life made up of years of study, of effort, but also of carefree freedom and new experiences. They were years, above all, of friendship. These friendships remained imprinted in the minds, in the memories, and on the faces of all those persons whom he met and came to know. There was an incredible variety of characters among his classmates.

Banas, for example, was superrich, while Bojes was the son of a poor miner. Some were politically active like Bernas and Kogler, while Romanski and Kus were among the most studious. And then there were the athletes: Kesek and Silkowski, not to mention Zweig, of course, the best soccer player in Wadowice and, like Selinger, a Jew. There were also two anti-Semites, Zmuda and Politwka. Politwka was always arguing with Kluger about the leading role that the Jews, in his opinion, had played in the Bolshevik revolution. And Czuprynski, how could they ever forget Czuprynski? Tall, elegant, likable, a boaster and great Don Juan—he certainly never failed to catch people's eye.

As for the professors, they were all extremely serious, but superb educators. Klimczyk, who taught Polish, often took his students to the theater. Heriadin taught natural sciences, and apologized every time he had to give a bad grade. Gebhardt, the professor of history, had an intellectual air and was pro-socialist. Every May 1 he wore his red tie. And then there were the two professors of Greek, first Damasiewicz, very slight but a tremendous character, and then Szeliski, who was an outright clown. The boys played incredible, sometimes even sadistic, tricks on him, such as putting glue in the sleeves on his overcoat or nailing his galoshes to the floor. But he didn't hold it against them. "They're just boys," he would say, and always ended up excusing and forgiving them.

Stopping off at church on his way to school, Karol was the last one to arrive every morning, with his face red and his hair—which he now wore long—permanently disheveled.

He got along well in class. He liked his classmates. He was the most prepared and earned the best grades. Yet he wasn't a "grind," and he didn't put on airs; he was like the others. He too did imitations of the teachers, especially Szeliski. He played goalie in soccer; he was nicknamed "Martyna" after a famous player. And, like the others, twice every month he went to dancing lessons along with the students from the girls' high school.

The only difference between Karol and his classmates was that he led a more intense religious life—and he was much more reserved. He often stayed home, among other things, to keep his father company. Another misfortune had struck the Wojtylas: Edmund, who was a doctor in another city, had died. He had caught scarlet fever from a patient and died after suffering for a long time and in excruciating agony.

Karol adored his brother. He always remembered how, at the age of ten, he had gone with his father to the Jagellonian University in Cracow for Edmund's graduation. Edmund's death left Karol prostrate, much more so than his mother's had. He was older now; he understood his own feelings and the emotions that he was going through. He found comfort in the spiritual help provided by a young priest who taught religion in his school, Don Kazimierz Figlewicz. He also took refuge in his passion for the theater—a passion that he felt gradually welling up within him during those school years.

He read the fathers of Polish romanticism, from Sienkiewicz to Slowacki, from Mickiewicz to Krasinski. But the author he loved the most was Cyprian Norwid. He preferred Norwid because of his nondenominational Christianity, which was capable of getting to the quintessence of the faith, and because of the great attention he paid to human beings as persons. And, above all, it was from the "knight of truth," as the poet defined himself, that Karol learned to love his homeland: it was a love that instead of reducing itself to myopic and narrow-minded nationalism, was projected over the universal horizon of history.

The classics were not the only things that urged Karol toward the dramatic arts. On the floor above the Wojtylas lived the Beers, a Jewish family who had a daughter, named Ginka, who was two years older than Karol. She was a beauty, slender with splendid black eyes. She was primarily studying medicine, but she also went out for theater; and, therefore, she was the first "teacher" of her young neighbor whom she immediately realized had talent.

Sometime later there was also Mieczyslaw Kotlarczyk, a professor of Polish literature who also taught directing and who dreamed of giving life to a theater of the inner word. Under his guidance, Karol came to the forefront as a director and actor. In the performances put on by the school's theater club he was paired up with Halina, the daughter of the president of the boys' high school. On one occasion, he even surpassed his own personal expectations: a colleague unexpectedly failed to show up for Slowacki's *Balladyna*, and Karol played two parts at once, both the "good" character and the villain.

This was the life of the young people of Wadowice, more or less the same as in other provincial Polish cities in the mid 1930s. It was a simple, tranquil life, even if it was governed by very precise rules that had to be rigorously obeyed. The behavior of the adults displayed obvious indications of the Puritanism that was typical of Habsburg society.

Just like many other localities, there was a lovers' lane where boys and girls met for rendezvous and, occasionally, slipped into an embrace or stole an innocent kiss. But woe be it to those who were discovered by their parents or, worse yet, by a teacher. They ran the risk of undergoing a pitiless interrogation and being loaded down with extra homework for an entire month.

Meanwhile, threatening clouds were gathering over Poland. A powerful wave of anti-Semitism from Germany was spreading through the central and northeastern parts of the country. This came along precisely in the period when Poland had just granted refuge to thousands of Jews who had been driven out by the Nazi regime.

Marshall Pilsudski had concentrated power in his hands, even though he maintained a system of parliamentary democracy. But once the man who had been called the "uncle of the Jews" and their protector was in his grave, Pilsudski's power passed over to a group of quarrelsome and ineffective colonels.

Parliament was soon dominated by a single force, the party of National Reunification, which had totalitarian tendencies and supported Nazi-style racism.

At the universities, especially those in Warsaw and Leopoli (Lviv), the Jewish students were subjected to severe discrimination; and four of them lost their lives as a result of the attacks they were continually forced to endure.

Then came the economic boycotts, which were actually considered to be indications of patriotism exerted against Jewish businesses, offices, and doctors, to prevent people from patronizing them. In Polish it was called *Owszem*: this became the watchword for the most extremist groups.

The young "thugs" of the National Radical Organization, who came from outside, tried doing their antics in Wadowice as well. But their picketing failed because the people reacted against it. Hardened as they were, the troublemakers wouldn't let that go by without retribution. They returned under the cover of night to smash storefronts and break windows. This time, however, the whole city took it as an insult.

During this period, feelings were quick to erupt in Karol's classes. There were heated discussions about Germany's intervention in the Spanish Civil War and above all about the Anschluss, when Austria tamely and connivingly submitted to Hitler.

If, however, the conflicts between Jews and anti-Semites could in one way or another be switched off at school, they immediately exploded again out on the soccer field. At the first opportunity, the Jew-baiters began to commit deliberate fouls, to insult and spit at them. "Give it to the Jew!" they would cry, as someone beat up his fallen adversary. Some of the boys would come in to make peace, but it got increasingly more difficult to interrupt those furious disputes.

The morning after the raid on the Jews, Professor Gebhardt entered the classroom with a black look. For a long time he kept silent. Then, barely able to speak, he said that what had

happened was not only outrageous, but completely contrary to
Polish tradition. He opened a book and began to read a passage
from the political manifesto that Mickiewicz had prepared in
1848 for the constitution of the future independent Slavic states.
Gebhardt articulated these words one by one:

> In the nation, everyone is a citizen. All the citizens are
> equal before the law and before the administration. To
> Israel "'—and that means the Jew,' the professor ex-
> plained," to our eldest brother, belong respect and help
> on the path to eternal good and welfare and equal rights
> in all matters....

But some Jews couldn't stand this persecution any longer.
Ginka had been expelled from the faculty of medicine at Cracow
simply because she was friends with a girl whose boyfriend was
a communist; and for that reason her family had decided to
leave for Palestine.

Karol and Jerzy went to say good-bye to her, but when they
saw that she was utterly shaken, her eyes glistening with tears,
they couldn't even manage to open their mouths. Instead, the
"Captain" spoke: "All Poles aren't anti-Semites—I'm not one,
you know this, don't you, Ginka?" She was glad to hear those
words, yet she frankly replied: "Yes, but there really aren't many
Poles like you." They accompanied her to the train in better
spirits. Fortunately Ginka had a strong character. She would
manage to overcome that trial too.

The year 1938 had begun, and the general situation in the
country continued to worsen. In Wadowice, by contrast, and
probably because of the reaction prompted by the anti-Jewish
provocations, the tension relaxed. Among the boys at school,
tensions relaxed as well. Over and above everything else, important events were on the horizon.

On the first of May, the archbishop of Cracow, Adam Stefan
Sapieha, came to administer the sacrament of confirmation; and

it was Karol, the best student in the *gymnasium* who was to deliver the welcoming address. Then, at the end of the month, came the final examinations, which practically everyone passed. Even Jerzy made it: peeking from behind Karol's shoulders, he had been able to check his Latin translation and correct it.

For the graduates, as always, there would be the grand ball, the *Komers,* held at the club for government functionaries, and also the most elegant site in town frequented by the upper middle class. The hall was decorated, and a very popular band was hired.

Then, however, there was a hitch. At the party, though there hadn't been any special knowledge of this beforehand, a group of young lawyers appeared, *en masse*, along with the officials of the Twelfth Regiment. They proceeded, as the dance began, to proposition all the female students.

Then, sensing that a storm was brewing, both the military and lawyers retreated in good order. The graduating students reclaimed the field. Elegant, with pomaded hair, white shirts, and ties, long pants, some even with gaiters, they proved first-rate at every dance: polonaises, mazurkas, waltzes, and even tangos, which had seemed so difficult in the practice sessions. It really was a terrific party.

Karol and Halina, dancing together, agreed to meet in Cracow, where they would continue to do theater. For others, it was a time for good-byes; they would take different paths, and who knew when they would meet again?

For everyone, however, it seemed to be the beginning of a happy time, full of novelty. Those young people hoped that Poland would escape the storm that was about to burst over their heads. As Wyspianksi had written, many years before, in one of his poems:

> Let the whole world be at war
> As long as the Polish countryside is tranquil,
> As long as the Polish countryside is at peace.

Chapter Three

SEPTEMBER 1, 1939

The cathedral was immense in the silence and barely illuminated by the sun, which was still weak and hidden by the clouds. Every now and then, one could hear a whispering in Latin at the altar in the north nave, which was dominated by a large black crucifix. It was there, in front of that crucifix, that Hedwig—the queen from the era of Poland's greatest splendor, the Jagellonian dynasty—used to come to pray every day.

On this day, just as he did on every first Friday of the month, Karol ascended the Wawel to make his confession to Don Figlewicz, who had now become his spiritual advisor and to also serve his Mass.

"How strange," Karol thought, as he looked around. The cathedral was deserted. At that time of day, there was always *somebody* there; now even the usual elderly ladies were gone.

Suddenly, the ground shuddered. Explosions were coming from far away, perhaps from the outskirts of Cracow; but the rumble echoed mightily all the way up to the top of the hill that overlooks the Vistula River.

Don Figlewicz spun around, and his glance met the terrified face of his altar boy. The sirens began to wail, and the first bursts of the antiaircraft guns were heard. For an instant, even the imposing mausoleum of Saint Stanislas, the martyr-bishop, seemed to be shaking.

You could tell from his hunched shoulders that the priest was also afraid. But Don Figlewicz didn't interrupt the Mass—though from that moment on he began to rush everything, first the gestures, then the prayers as well. It was September 1, 1939. "That day," Karol said, "will never be erased from my memory." Adolf Hitler had unleashed his blitzkrieg, his "lightning war," his massive surprise attack. Officially, he just wanted to annex the city of Danzig and its famous "corridor." But, in fact, he planned to cross Poland and seize the oil fields of Romania and the breadbasket of Ukraine. In the end, he also planned to realize his grand ambition of conquering Europe.

Members of the government in Warsaw had a share in the blame for this: they hadn't believed the German threats, at least not until Czechoslovakia had been occupied and transformed into the Protectorate of Bohemia and Moravia. The Western allies were also at fault; for too long they had hesitated to send strong and credible signals to dissuade Berlin from any rash moves.

"Die for Danzig?" French deputy Marcel Déat asked in a newspaper article. The question was brimming with criminal indifference, even as it took his readers' "No!" for granted. Abandoned once more, Poland went off to face its ineluctably sad destiny.

Thus, at dawn on September 1, 1939, the monstrous Nazi war machine was set into motion: a million and a half men. At 4:49 A.M., the armed divisions of the Wehrmacht, the German army, invaded the territory of Poland and stormed ahead, mile after mile, while the artillery poured out its nonstop barrage and the planes of the Luftwaffe dropped death and destruction from the skies. Of Poland's five hundred military aircraft, only one barely got off the ground; the rest were blown up where they were parked.

Meanwhile, back in the cathedral, the Mass had ended. Don

Figlewicz and Karol rushed out onto the open square of the Wawel and saw the German bombers drop their murderous load on the plainly visible targets: the barracks on Warszawska Street, the ammunition dump, the railroad, and the radio station. The inferno came and went before Polish anti-aircraft guns hit a single enemy plane.

Karol left with a shout: "My father's at home!" He barely said good-bye to his priest friend and set off on a mad dash along the streets which were filled with smoke. Some buildings were on fire. The ambulances couldn't make their way through the flood of panic-stricken people who had poured out of their houses.

Finally, he reached the Debniki quarter and 10 Tyniecka Street: the gate, the garden, and the squat gray block of flats where he lived with his father. Some of their relatives had offered them that dark, damp basement apartment; it was certainly better than nothing. The Wojtylas had been able to move from Wadowice to Cracow. Karol had registered in the Jagellonian University and had begun to take courses in Polish philology (similar to linguistics).

He sped down the last steps and practically crashed into the "Captain," who hugged him tightly. The "Captain" had also been worried: "Where were you? I looked for you everywhere." "But Papa," Karol said, "don't you remember? I went to the Wawel, to Don Figlewicz."

An agitated voice was heard coming from the radio, announcing the latest news of the Nazi invasion and the declaration of war: "The German government has proclaimed the annexation of Danzig to the Reich."

At more or less the same time, Hitler was issuing a declaration to his army, saying exactly the opposite. Every word was, of course, false. "The Polish State has refused to regulate our relations in a peaceful way, as I desired, and has had recourse to arms. A series of violations at the frontier..." and so on.

To justify his aggression against Poland, the Führer, Adolph

Hitler, continued imperturbably to maintain that the enemy had attacked the German radio station at Gleiwitz. Actually, the assault had been carried out by the infamous German special police force, the SS, who were wearing Polish uniforms.

Juliusz Kydrynksi, a university classmate of Karol's, arrived all out of breath. He begged Karol to help him pull the cart with his family's household furnishings. They hadn't gone half a mile when a German fighter plane broke away from the trail of the bombers, turned back, and began to machine-gun everything that moved in the streets. The two boys managed to take refuge in a large building, but they were frightened to death.

Karol ran home; he didn't want to leave his father alone any longer. With some difficulty, he convinced Karol, Sr., to leave the city—not by train, because that would risk an attack from the air, but on foot, as almost everyone else was doing.

They had to go eastward, away from the Germans. Even the radio, although for different reasons, confirmed that same option. "All men with call-up notices," the speaker said, "must head east to present themselves to the units they belong to."

Throwing a few necessities into a suitcase, Karol and his father went off on the road to Tarnow. There was an endless stream of people, many of them Jews. Many peasant families gradually joined the march, bringing everything they owned with them—even their animals, cows, horses, chickens, and geese. The young people tried to keep their morale up, telling funny stories and singing, while the elders were already regretting they had undertaken the hasty journey without thinking it over and, above all, without a set destination.

The "Captain" had a hard time walking, and his pace became slower and slower. Karol supported him, all but dragging him along. A military truck loaded with munitions pulled alongside, and Karol talked the driver into giving his father a ride. It was a piece of luck, but it only lasted as far as Tarnow where the driver decided to stop. There was no point, he said, in going any further; he would never catch up with the officers in charge of the division to drop off his load.

Some soldiers said that on September 4, the Nazis had taken possession of the Danzig "corridor." There had been a bloodbath: German tanks with their terrifying long-distance firing capacity pitted against the light cavalry of the Pomorska brigade, armed with nothing but their long ceremonial weapons.

Two days later Cracow was also occupied. Though the news came as no surprise, it was a harsh blow for these people. It meant having to cut off their links to what was dearest to them: their homes, their relatives, and their jobs. Above all, the supplies of bread had run out. Drinking water was gone as well; even the puddles along the highway had all dried up. All they could see were the immense fields of potatoes. No one wanted to sing or laugh anymore. People were heard cursing and lamenting. There was an air of increasing desperation.

At first, it was barely audible, but the buzzing got louder and more threatening as it drew near. Some of the people took refuge beneath the trees and in the ditches. But the men and women who shielded their children with their bodies stayed put, defenseless, serving as targets for the bestial fury of the German dive bombers, the Stukas, in their screaming nose-dives as they left behind them a long wake of blood and death.

The survivors—Karol had saved his father by dragging him onto an escarpment—remained petrified when faced with the terrible, ghastly scene. There was nothing they could do except bury a few poor bodies. Then they had to move on, hoping that they really would find safety in the east. They took to the road again; but the "Captain" was now completely exhausted.

In another city, Rzeszow, they learned that practically all thirty-five of the Polish divisions had been destroyed. The few divisions that were still resisting had been caught in a pincer movement by enemy troops. Midnight of September 8 passed, and an armed German division arrived at the suburbs of Warsaw.

The refugees continued to march for a few more days, until
the winding curve of a river appeared in the distance: it was the
San. They had walked for one hundred twenty miles; they were
dead tired, but happy. They could now stop for a little while
and rest.

They had scarcely spread out in a meadow when some Polish soldiers appeared: starving, dressed like ragamuffins; their
units had been disbanded. They reported how the Red Army
had crossed the eastern frontier on the morning of September
17 under the pretext of aiding their Ukrainian and Byelorussian
"brothers," who were living in Polish territory and were "threatened" by Germany. In reality, it had been an out-and-out invasion of Poland.

The agreement signed a month before by Ribbentrop and
Molotov, by Nazi Germany and communist Russia, was, in the
official version, a "nonaggression pact" between the two powers. But there had also been a series of secret protocols attached,
one of which laid out the division of Poland into two "spheres
of influence," precisely demarcated by three rivers: the Narew,
the San, and the Vistula.

The Kremlin was worried by the speed with which the German troops had crossed Poland. Hence, the invasion by the Red
Army was meant to be an explicit call to its advancing ally to
scrupulously observe the line of demarcation that they had agreed
upon and signed in the secret clauses of their pact.

Thus, from that point on, they proceeded in complete syn-
chrony. The Soviet Union took the eastern part, representing 52
percent of the Polish territory. Germany got the provinces of
Lublin and Warsaw, along with a few zones of the western region that were directly incorporated into the Third Reich. The
rest was transformed into the "General Government," with
Cracow as its center.

For the fourth time, as in the days of the German kings and
the Russian tsars, but now under far more ruthless systems,
Germany and Russia agreed to divide up the Polish nation, which

simply disappeared—along with Czechoslovakia and Austria— from the map of Europe. Unfortunately, there was now no denying that the war, the second great war of the twentieth century, had at long last broken out.

On Sunday, September 3, 1939, two days after the invasion of Poland, first England and then France sent an ultimatum to Germany. For all practical purposes, there ultimatums were a declaration of war. Nevertheless, many people thought there might still be some wiggle room left to block the conflict or at least to find a compromise acceptable to both sides.

But on the evening of that same Sunday, at 9 P.M., an irreparable step was taken. The German fleet went on the attack. Without any warning, the submarine *U-30* torpedoed and sank the English ocean liner *Athenia*, two hundred miles west of the Hebrides. Aboard the ship, which was headed from Montreal to Liverpool, were 1,400 passengers; 112 of them including 28 Americans were lost. And with that the last hope for peace died.

The Polish refugees, like Karol and his father, who had arrived at the San River, knew nothing about what was happening in the rest of Europe, or even in the rest of the world. Perhaps for this very reason, because they were unaware of any of these events, they decided to retrace the one hundred twenty miles they had covered on foot. They would return to Cracow, where they hoped to find at least a roof over their heads, some refuge, and, above all, safety.

Chapter Four

HITLER'S "NEW ORDER"

Cracow no longer seemed to be the same city. It was unrecognizable, as if a painter had covered it with a coat of dark gray; or, worse, as if around the city, and the whole country, they had raised the bars of an immense prison.

Even from a distance, as he returned from the pointless flight to the east with his father, Karol had noticed that radical change. The Wawel, of all places, had become the unhappy symbol of the *Neue Ordnung*, the "new order" that Hitler was imposing on Poland. He didn't simply want to wipe it out as a nation and a state, but wanted to strike at its heart, to stamp out its soul, and strangle its culture, and erase its historical memory.

On the bastion of Sandomierz flew a banner with the swastika, the symbol of Nazi Germany. The cathedral had been closed; Archbishop Sapieha had managed to celebrate the last Mass on September 19. And in the castle, the ancient home of the Polish kings, the Piasts, the Jagellonians, there now resided Hans Frank, the governor general.

When he had taken possession of the castle, he had entered by the main gate, which was adorned by a Latin inscription, *"Si Deus Nobiscum, Quis Contra Nos?"* which translates: "If God is for us, who can be against us?" There couldn't be a more blatant, more strident, and more tragically symbolic contrast.

22

Frank was an intellectual, the father of five children, and—apparently benevolent, conciliatory, civil, and a great lover of music. But in reality, he was a ruthless, bloody man, an authentic criminal, an assassin.

The day after his installation, he had said: "The Poles must be the slaves of the German Reich. They have no rights. Their only duty is to obey, to do what we order them to do. They must be continuously reminded that their duty is obedience...."

This state of subjection very quickly became the normal, daily condition of the population. At night there was a curfew. German patrols fired, on sight, the moment anyone tried to run away or didn't stop when told to, or didn't jump aside as quickly as possible when the military passed by. In the daytime, there were continual, stifling inspections on the streets: anyone without a pass was arrested immediately and deported to a laager or work camp.

The marketplace was the heart of the old city. At its center is still the *Sukiennice*, the ancient commercial quarter, famous all over Europe. On one side rises the church of Saint Mary, flanked by two towers. From the taller of the two, a trumpet blast resounds, every hour on the hour, brusquely interrupted after a few notes. This is in memory of the legend of the sentinel, killed by an arrow to the throat as he was sounding the alarm at the arrival of the Tartar invaders.

And now the new barbarians had arrived. They had turned the square upside down, destroying the statue of the great poet Adam Mickiewicz and rifling from the *Mariacka*, the stupendous wooden altar piece by Wit Stwosz, which they later took to Nuremberg. With all that devastation Cracow felt disfigured and physically violated, right to its very core.

But the number one emergency, obviously, was food. According to the governor general, the Poles could get along perfectly well on six hundred fifty calories a day, as opposed to the two thousand allotted to the subjects of the Reich. In a word, the Poles were "cheap slaves," as Hitler himself had suggested.

For that reason, the Germans had their own special stores (*nur für Deutsche*) well stocked with all sorts of goods, meats, fresh vegetables, and butter, items which were obtainable nowhere else, while the Poles had to stand in long, long lines for a measly bread ration. Once during this time Frank insisted upon being invited to the archbishop's palace, whereupon Archbishop Sapieha served up what was dinner for the majority of the population: stale bread, a little potatoes, and ersatz coffee.

Karol too got out of bed at around four in the morning, when the streets were still frozen, and queued up to buy half a round loaf, which was often stale anyway. But for sugar, margarine, and especially coal—the winter that year was a harsh one, and the first snows had already begun to fall—you had to turn to the black market. But that was risky because if you were caught, you wound up on the list of the deportees.

Despite this risk, you had to adapt to the situation; you had to survive by exploiting the margins of freedom, however narrow, that the regime still left open, whether it really intended to do so or not.

Karol registered for his second year at the university, managing to take his examination in contemporary Polish with Professor Nitsch. Then, something that was possible only in private homes, an intense cultural activity developed. He went to the house of Juliusz Kydrynski to talk with his friends about literature and the theater. He often went to the villa overlooking the Vistula owned by the Szkockis, where they had evenings of music and poetry readings.

But Hitler's "new order" had more than mere repression in mind. Frank had clearly explained this to his subordinates: they had to get rid of the intellectuals, thereby preventing them from becoming a ruling class. That meant sweeping away the clergy, the nobility, and the Jews. The program that he sketched out was so dreadful that it went far beyond any of the "ethnic cleansing" we have seen in our time.

"Every trace of Polish culture," he said, "must be eradicated. Poles with a Nordic appearance will be brought to Germany to work in our factories. The children with Nordic looks will be taken away from their parents and raised as German workers. The rest? They'll work. They won't eat much. And in the end they'll die. There will never again be a Poland."

On November 6, 1939, the German authorities convened all the professors and academic personnel of the Jagellonian University. Supposedly this was to discuss programs, but it was a trap. The one hundred eighty-three professors who showed up, including old Nitsch, were arrested and deported to the concentration camp at Sachsenhausen. Later, in response to strong international pressures, a hundred or so would be released; but the others never returned.

The *Sonderkaktion Krakau* (Special Action Cracow), as the operation was designated, represented the peak of the assault on the Polish intelligentsia, an attack that the Nazis also inanely labeled an "extraordinary pacification action." High schools, universities, newspapers, and artistic associations were closed; libraries were destroyed. The Slowacki Theater was renamed and reserved for the Germans. Even the works of Chopin and other composers were banned. Then it was the Church's turn: priests were arrested, celebrations of the feast days of the nation's patron saints were prohibited, and all church property was expropriated.

Finally they came for the Jews.

To make room for German citizens in the provinces annexed by the Reich, a massive deportation was carried out: 1.2 million Poles, judged "unassimilable," and 300 thousand Jews were uprooted from their homes and forcefully removed to the east. The General Government—where more than three million Jews were already living—thus became an ideal "laboratory" for setting up what the Nazi leaders, hatching their plans in deep secrecy, had agreed to call the "Final Solution" or the extermination of the Jewish people.

In Cracow the Jews had their own sector, called Kazimierz,

to the south of the city. There, at least early on, they were left in
relative peace. But as soon as they stepped outside their boundaries, the discrimination and harassment began. They were
forced to wear an armband with the Star of David on it. Some
store owners put up signs saying: "Jews and dogs forbidden to
enter." In this way, exposed to public scorn and outlawed, they
were now considered *Untermenschen*, subhumans.

Frank had been excused from dealing directly with the Jewish question, but he wanted to do his part anyway. And he spelled
things out clearly to his immediate coworkers: "Gentlemen, I
must ask you to get rid of all feelings of compassion. We must
annihilate the Jews!"

A few months later, at Oswiecim, which the Germans called
Auschwitz, some forty miles from Cracow, a concentration camp
was opened. Actually, people said, it was a "quarantine camp."
It was initially reserved for political prisoners who were to be
treated with particular harshness. Later, however, it would be
used for something else, something that only a criminal mind
could have devised.

Meanwhile, in the part of Poland it had occupied, the Soviet Union was not far behind the Nazis in repressiveness. Of
the twelve million inhabitants, at least one and a half million
were deported to Siberia and locked up in "re-education camps"—
enormous clusters of wooden huts, where it was extremely cold—
and they were subject to cruel treatment day and night.

And then there was the Katyn massacre.

The eastern territories, controlled by Russia, were also home
to about 250 thousand Polish military men who were considered prisoners of war—in a war, it may be noted, that had never
been declared. The great majority of these officers were not career soldiers but reservists: by day they were professors, doctors, journalists, teachers, and intellectuals. All of them, in the
eyes of the Kremlin, were potential leaders of the resistance,
ready to fight for the rebirth of an independent Poland.

On March 5, 1940, the Politburo ordered the shooting of

at least 22 thousand officers who were labeled "inveterate and incorrigible enemies of Soviet power." The slaughter was carried out in the Katyn forest, and many of the bodies were then thrown into common graves. Immediately afterwards, 61 thousand of the victims' family members were transferred, so to speak, to Kazakhstan.

For years afterwards, not only Moscow—which might be understandable in some ways—but even the British government continued to blame that barbarous massacre on the Germans.

In Warsaw, as in Cracow, all this was as yet unknown. But the Poles realized that they had been caught in a lethal vise. Karol, as well, was in agony. History, tragic history, had suddenly burst into his country, into his own private life; and he was overwhelmed by it. He felt as if his hopes and his future had been cheated. He was only twenty years old—how his existence had changed in such a short time!

He began reading not just the classics, not just his favorite authors, but everything he could get his hands on. He wrote two long plays, *Job* and *Jeremiah,* and some very fine poems, one of which he dedicated to the memory of his mother. He studied French. He gave Latin lessons to a younger friend, Mieczyslaw Malinski. He also delivered take-out meals for a restaurant.

His days were so full and frenetic, precisely because he was trying to forget that enormous explosion of evil. But he couldn't do it; it was impossible to remain outside of it all.

Kotlarczyk, his director friend, was stuck in Wadowice; and they had arrested two of the director's brothers. In a letter he wrote, Karol expressed his own sense of solidarity, but also the pain he felt over the martyrdom of his homeland. "The idea of Poland lived in us," he wrote, "just as it had for the generation of the Romantics. But in truth this Poland no longer existed, now that the peasants were being beaten and imprisoned because they had laid claim to their undeniable political rights, because they felt the hour of destiny had come, because they were right...."

The bitterness of these words was primarily, and above all, derived from a doubt that was gnawing within him. That is, young Wojtyla wondered if Poland hadn't collapsed solely on account of the bestial fury of the Nazis, but rather because the Poles themselves might have been somewhat at fault: the ruling classes and the political parties had scorned twenty years of independence and freedom, thinking more about their own power than about building and strengthening the democracy.

It was clear that he leaned toward the second hypothesis. "The nation," he wrote, "was betrayed and deceived." But, in the end, he still managed to find, thanks to his religious faith, the path of hope: "I believe that our liberation must be the door of Christ." These were more or less the same words that Karol would pronounce again, many years later.

Chapter Five

EXPERIENCE AS A WORKER

Halfway through 1940 the war took a strange twist—a strange and dangerous twist.

Apparently, at the beginning, the idyll between Germany's Hitler and Russia's Stalin had apparently not soured. There hadn't been any friction between their plans for conquest. Then a new development came about that would cast doubt on the solidity of the pact, and especially on the honesty of those who had signed it—always assuming, of course, that one can use such language in the case of two ruthless dictators.

German troops had gone from victory to victory. On April 19, operation *Weserübung*, the invasion of Denmark and Norway, had been unleashed. The two governments had been warned in time about the risk they were running, but they didn't believe it. Meanwhile, if the Norwegians had taken even the most elementary of security measures, and had its army been in a condition to defend itself, the Second World War might have taken a rather different turn at this point in history.

Then, with dazzling speed and ease, Holland, Belgium, and France were conquered in only five days. Leopold III, the young Belgian king, in a decision that many of his compatriots would never forgive him for, surrendered on May 28. At Dunkirk, the Allies, incredibly, managed to evacuate the more than 300 thousand soldiers who were caught in a trap. But the French army proved to be practically nonexistent. On June 14, the Eighteenth Army of General Kuchler entered Paris; on the Eiffel Tower they had raised the swastika.

Hitler didn't even have the time to savor his success. The day afterwards the first bad news had arrived: the Red Army was occupying Lithuania, despite the fact that the Lithuanian government had accepted the Russian ultimatum and all the conditions laid down by Moscow. Another twenty-four hours passed, and with the usual quasi-bureaucratic mechanism of ultimatum, the invasion took place, the same fate that befell Latvia and then Estonia. Within two months, after the manipulated election of the respective Parliaments, the three Baltic states would be officially "absorbed" by Russia.

Obviously, this was not a simple coincidence. In fact, while the Führer was busied with the campaign in the west and his plans to invade Great Britain, Stalin had cynically seized the occasion to lay the foundations for his own future empire. Then, as if all this were a minor detail, he informed his ally that he had been forced to undertake such an annexation in order to put an end to the repeated British and French attempts to sow discord between Germany and the Soviet Union.

Hitler exploded in fury. He had never felt so humiliated, so taken for a ride. He would become all the more embittered when, after the Battle of Britain had been lost, despite the furious bombardment of London and other cities, he would see himself constrained to put the invasion off to an undetermined date. It was just at that moment that, partly out of rage and retaliation, and partly for reasons of security, he decided to intensify the repression in all the occupied countries.

In Poland as well there was a brutal turning of the screw. The inspections became more rigid and systematic. The beatings, the arrests, the deportations—and the summary executions—increased.

For some months now, in the territories of the General Government, forced labor had been imposed upon all healthy men from the age of fourteen (twelve, in the case of Jews) to seventy. Before this, anyone who was found to be without a job could be sent to Germany for forced labor; now anyone caught without documents could be killed immediately.

For this reason, like many other young men, Karol had to get a "work card," an *Arbeitskarte*. That way, he would be able not just to keep his ration card, which he needed to eat, not just scrape together a salary, even if a very small one, which was indispensable once his father's pension was suspended; but above all, he would avoid the danger of being stopped one day and, without having time to explain, shot right in the middle of the street.

Karol's friends found him a job in the Zakrzowek quarry, which was part of the giant Solvay chemical operations. Juliusz Kydrynski was there, too, along with some other university classmates.

It was a safe job that the Nazis had a hard time keeping tabs on. The quarry bosses were Poles, people who could be trusted. Besides, the workers knew that the "students," as they called those youngsters, were not potential competitors for their jobs. Once the war was over, they would go back to their books.

And so Karol began to work at Zakrzowek. Every day he walked the two-mile route in a half hour. In good weather, it was even pleasant, but in winter, with the temperatures often plunging to well below zero, you risked frostbite and had to rub your face with petroleum jelly. He and Juliusz, at the lunch break, slipped into a hut, where they could, at the very least, take shelter from the frozen sleet that pierced them to the bone. In this hut, there was a little stove; and they could even warm up some coffee.

The quarry was a huge well, a sort of canyon; with walls that were sixty to ninety feet high, and when you stood down inside it, you could see nothing else, only the rock, unless you bent back and looked up towards the sky.

Their work was organized in a rough assembly line. Some workers chopped blocks of limestone to pieces; others collected the fragments of stone with big pitchforks to dump into wheelbarrows, still others pushed the wheelbarrows all the way to the rail line.

Karol's first job was as a "laborer." He wore dark red overalls, several sizes too large, wooden clogs, and a cap that was soon smeared with motor oil stains. He went up and down, from the quarry to the rail line, with a wheelbarrow full of crushed stones which he then dumped into the little cars that rode to the kiln for processing. This went on for eight hours, including mealtime, from 6 A.M. to 2 P.M., which was the first of the three shifts. But, like everyone else, he had to take his place in the regular rotation.

Sometimes he was called in to replace another worker, to break up the limestone blocks, for example; and he had to be very careful—as the old timers warned him—about getting chips in his eyes. But in general, the "students" were assigned to easier jobs. And Karol, joking about it, wrote to a friend who was concerned about him: "Don't worry! So far I haven't had to break rocks."

Then there was the great leap. Only three months had gone by, and he was promoted to be the assistant to the blaster, who had the job with the greatest responsibility—and risk. The master artificer (blaster) would make a hole in the mass of limestone, insert the explosive charge with a long pole, and finally detonate it.

The master's name was Franciszek Labus, and he was very cordial with the young Karol. In fact, seeing the progress the young man had made, Labus allowed him to perform the difficult operation on his own; limiting himself to checking on the fact that Karol had done everything properly. And once, for no particular reason, he came out with a strange remark: "You know, you ought to become a priest. You'll sing well, because you have a fine voice, and you'll do well...."

At the time, Karol wasn't thinking of the priesthood. Nevertheless, during those years he had an experience that at first—for him, an intellectual who had been turned overnight into a *robotnik* (worker)—had certainly been difficult, onerous, and even traumatic, but that left a deep mark on his human and spiritual destiny, on his whole future.

As a matter of fact, thanks precisely to his having experienced the working conditions, he learned the Gospel afresh. He learned the value of solidarity, particularly in moments of suffering, pain, and injustice. He discovered the harshness and fatigue of work, but at the same time—as he wrote in a poem—he also discovered the dignity and greatness of work that is within the human being, because it belongs to the very essence, to the nature of man's humanity.

> Listen, the steady rhythm of the hammers, so familiar,
> I cast it into men, to test the force of every blow.
> Listen, an electrical charge cuts the river of rock,
> and a thought grows in me, from day to day:
> all the greatness of work lies within the man.

He often had recourse to poetry, because he found it to be the most natural way to express his feelings and, above all, reflect upon the great mystery that humans represented for him: the person in flesh and bone who confronts his own freedom and Christian hope, the person who has come to grips with the great questions of existence, with all the trials that he must undergo, but also with the certainty that good will prevail in the end, and thus, that life is a season that is worth living.

Karol was stunned by a tragic accident in the quarry: the death of a fellow worker when a rock chip from a dynamite explosion pierced his temple. He recalled the scene this way:

> They lifted up the body. They marched in silence.
> It still emanated fatigue and a sense of injustice...

They laid him out on his back on a sheet of gravel.
The wife came, grief-stricken.
The child came back from School...

Looking at that poor body Karol felt great sorrow, but also
something very much like powerlessness and, along with that,
anger. In the end, however, he managed to understand.

The rocks move again.
The hopper disappears among the flowers.
Once again an electrical charge cuts into the quarry.
But the man has carried away with him
    the secret structure of the world
    where love gushes higher,
    the more it is filled with rage.

A year passed, and he was transferred to Borek Falecki, the
Solvay chemical plant. It was a longer trip from home, but in
the factory, where he was assigned to the water purification
department, at least they had a canteen that supplied hot soup
and a few pieces of bread to dunk in it. Plus, the job was con-
siderably lighter, with more breaks.

Karol often chose the night shift because, that way, he didn't
have to shoulder the pails of calcium hydroxide. His job was simply to keep an eye on the boiler. So he had a great deal of time to
read the books that he brought from home and, in the winter, he
could stay warm. In any event, he was a great worker. If any sort
of emergency came up, he never shirked his responsibilities.

The workers gave him a cordial welcome; and as they got
to know him, they gradually began to love him. They respected
him too; and they didn't harass him when he would kneel down
to pray in the middle of the workplace at noon. They even
brought him food if he couldn't leave his assignment; and if
they saw that he was tired on the night shift, they made him
rest. "Sleep a little," they said, "we'll take care of the boiler."

There was more than just work. Karol and his fellow workers often had heated discussions about all sorts of things, including religious problems. On that score, the expert was a certain Mankwoski, a tall, fat man, a member of the Polish Socialist party and a thorough atheist.

Chapter Six

WITHOUT A FATHER

T he last time they had taken a walk together, Karol and his father found themselves witnessing a very painful scene. A German patrol had come across two older Jews, easily recognizable by their armbands. Probably man and wife, they were holding hands. Pointing their guns at the couple's backs, the soldiers had forced the old people first to walk faster and then to run. The men sniggered as they insulted and threatened them: "Dirty Jews! You can't come here! You have to stay locked up where you belong!"

The "Captain" had been deeply affected and distressed by this. For days he had done nothing but tell everyone the story about what he had seen. He kept repeating: "The poor people! How can you treat human beings that way?!" And he grew still sadder when someone told him the rumors about deportations and concentration camps.

From that time on he wouldn't leave the house—not even to go to the literary evenings where his son recited the poems he had started writing around that time. The "Captain" excused himself, saying that he didn't want to have anymore ugly run-ins. But in fact he wasn't well. He felt enormous fatigue; he couldn't even handle the few household chores, not even cooking the little bit of potatoes that now made up their dinner.

In the factory, Karol had asked to work on the day shift. He preferred being home at night, when it was harder to find a doctor. He was anxious, seeing his father reduced to that condition, so different from how he used to be.

Ever since his mother had died, Karol had lived with his father in an almost absolute symbiosis, which nonetheless felt perfectly natural and spontaneous. He had discovered that fatherhood could be more than just biological; it was, above all, human and spiritual.

The "Captain" had never been an authoritarian father, not even a paternalistic or possessive one. His relationship with his son had always been marked by understanding, a willingness to listen, but also by firmness in guiding him along the path to adulthood. He had a strong sense of duty; if he was demanding with Karol, he was even more so with himself.

Karol owed a special debt of gratitude to his father for the way he had helped him to mature in his religious faith, without ever forcing him or setting conditions. After years and years, he would always remember the time when, getting up at the crack of dawn, he had found his father on his knees praying. It was an image that remained stamped in his eyes and in his heart.

Now those days seemed infinitely far away. His father no longer responded. He spent the whole day stretched out on his bed, as he did on that bitterly cold day of February 18, 1941.

When work was over, Karol went to the clinic to pick up some medicine. As usual, he stopped by the Kydrynski's house. Mrs. Kydrynski—by now Karol also called her "mama"—used to prepare supper for them. Her daughter, Maria, heated it up, and she offered to walk home with him to Tyniecka Street.

As they entered, Maria called out "Good evening, Captain," and went into the kitchen. Karol found his father in a strange position: he seemed to be resting, but he had slipped half-way out of the bed, as if he had been trying to get up. As he started to lift him, Karol felt that his father's hands were ice cold. He let out a cry, and Maria came running. She bent down to listen to his heart and realized that there was nothing to be done. She stood up and gently looked her friend in the eye.

The girl went to call a priest and her brother, Juliusz, but Karol didn't move from his father's bedside. On his knees, he held his father's hands and wept; he couldn't stop lamenting that he hadn't been there at the end. This same situation had already happened twice before, at the death of his mother and that of his brother, Edmund. It seemed to be his fate, an incomprehensible and cruel fate.

All throughout that night he kept watch over his father's body. "I'm all alone," he kept saying to Juliusz, who tried to comfort him and keep him company.

"At twenty I've already lost all the people I've loved!" he said in despair, but also perhaps with a touch of rage. He didn't just feel a sense of loss and insecurity at being deprived of the person who had always lived by his side, supported, and protected him. There was something far deeper, something like an uprooting from everything that his father represented, via origins, tradition, family history, and authority. It was like being violently ripped out of the soil in which he, the son, had grown until then.

In the blink of an eye, as if he were someone else, Karol began to talk in an excited, frenetic manner. He said that there was no time left for nostalgia, for forays into the past, not even for uncertainties. He had to confront reality. And, above all, he had to make a decision, a real decision.

Juliusz didn't understand; he thought Karol was referring to the theater. But he was talking more to himself than to his friend; and he meant a different choice, a choice that had always been in the background, overshadowed or supplanted by other experiences, by other perspectives, or unconsciously postponed because he didn't feel ready to take that step. But the death of his father had of necessity brought everything to the surface. It had instigated a process of detaching him from his earlier plans and making him more clearly see the path upon which he must enter.

The Kydrynski family made him come stay at their home for a while. That way, they thought, he wouldn't have to endure his suffering all by himself. However, Karol's life could no longer be what it used to be. From that moment on, other questions, other inner torments, began to arise.

So Karol's personal story had reached a moment of decision. But meanwhile, against the backdrop of Poland, Europe, and the world, a far more important story was being decided. The war had taken an unexpected and disastrous turn, pregnant with new and stormy consequences: Germany had attacked its former ally, the Soviet Union.

In his infinite presumption, Stalin had never believed the break would come. True, he had endangered the alliance by snatching as much as he could of eastern Europe, while the German army was busy on the western front. But he had never thought—and he had even told the British as much—that behind the Nazi expansion there might be any sort of threat to the Soviet Union, or even a serious danger for the whole European continent.

If Stalin wasn't thinking about this, Hitler was; and he had been for a long time. He had anticipated it some fifteen years before in *Mein Kampf*, where he wrote: "When we speak today of a new territory in Europe, we must think above all of Russia and the vassal states on its borders. It seems as if destiny itself wishes to point out these regions to us."

Hitler also closely linked the Russian question to the Jews. "The colossal empire of the east," he said, "is ripe for collapse; and the end of the Jewish domination in Russia will also be the end of Russia as a state."

The Führer had done more than spell this out in forceful and unequivocal terms. He had also demonstrated it with his increasingly aggressive strategy, which led to the occupation of Yugoslavia and Greece. If all that wasn't enough, shouldn't suspicions have been aroused by the concentration of thousands of troops just over the border from Russia in Romania and Bulgaria?

Nevertheless, when at 3:30 A.M. on Sunday, June 22, 1942, Operation Barbarossa was launched, and the armored battalions of the Wehrmacht crossed the Niemen River to pour into Soviet territory. Both the Kremlin and the Red Army were taken by surprise. Thousands of men had already been killed before the Russians had even managed to organize, if not a counteroffensive, at least some sort of resistance. Before they could take off, hundreds of Russian planes were destroyed as well.

Hitler had expressly told the commanders of the three armies: "The war against Russia will be the kind that can't be fought in a chivalrous fashion. This is a struggle between different ideologies and races, and will have to be conducted with an unprecedented harshness, cruelty, and ruthlessness." And it was. The objective was to wipe the Soviet Union from the face of the earth forever.

News of the conflict between Germany and Russia arrived in Poland, and some angles of the story got a positive reception. In fact, an accord had been reached between Stalin and the Polish government in exile: by its terms, the Poles would be allowed to fight in the army being organized by General Anders and not just in the Soviet armed forces. Apart from that, though, what could Poland hope for from a war between the two dictatorships that had already split up its territories like ravenous beasts?

Then, even assuming that one of the two powers would prevail in the end, what was there to wish for? To remain under Nazism, under its inhuman ferocity, of which Poland already had plenty of tragic experience? Or else to fall once more under the Russian tyranny, whose communist faction had already given notice that it was far more terrible than the czarist one?

In either case, Poland would lose. It would be headed for a shattered future. The suicide rate, which had sharply risen in those days, was surely a painful indication of that undeniable fact.

Perhaps for that very reason, so as not to think about the

horrifying abyss yawning before his homeland, Karol flung himself into work. He deliberately renewed his artistic and literary contacts, even though he now knew for certain that this would never be his ultimate destination in life.

Poland was trying to survive, while waiting to learn the result of that great clash. But above all, it was waiting to learn the name of the man who would be—and who could say for how long?—its future ruler and certain oppressor.

In only three weeks, the army of Field Marshal von Bock, with its thirty infantry divisions and fifteen divisions of tanks and motorized troops, had come within two hundred miles of Moscow. It was the same route that Napoleon had taken in 1812 when he set off for the Russian capital, after he also had crossed the Niemen—by an astonishing coincidence, on the same day: June 22. At the same time, two other German armies—one to the north, the other to the south—were advancing, respectively, toward the Baltic countries and Leningrad, and toward Kiev, the capital of Ukraine.

In Berlin, they were sure that this would be another lightning victory like the Polish campaign. Hitler was so convinced that Russia would now be liquidated that he had the head of his press office announce the news to foreign correspondents. At the peak of his arrogance, he gave precise orders why the surrender of Moscow, or Leningrad, would never be accepted, even if an offer were made. But could Operation Barbarossa be objectively described as though it was winding down?

At the very least, some of these signals should have led Hitler to a bit more caution. Contrary to what the Nazis expected, there had been no popular uprisings in Russia. Russian troops had begun organizing, fighting, and resisting. New Russian airplanes, once again, appeared out of nowhere and roared through the skies.

In Poland, there was an old saying: "When the Black Eagle heads east, he comes back with broken wings." The eagle meant Prussia, but the adage might turn out to have a new timeliness.

Chapter Seven

Words As Weapons

Thather evening, the performance would take place in a house on the left bank of the Vistula. It was better to keep changing locations and to choose an apartment as remote as possible from the previous one. That way, the Gestapo, the German state secret police under the Nazis, which must have had more than a few address lists, would have a harder time catching them red-handed.

The actors had already arrived some time before, just a few at a time. The same was true for the spectators, who were never more than fifteen or so: persons who were known, carefully picked, and expressly invited. Beyond that, you had to keep your eyes peeled so you didn't run into some patrol. If you were stopped after the curfew, you ran the risk of being deported to a concentration camp.

Not a single ray of light filtered through from the outside. The shutters had been hermetically sealed, and the windows screened. Even inside, in the living room, it was almost pitch black. There were only two lighted candles on a small table: that was all the set there was in this avant-garde theater. The decorations were reduced to a minimum. The supreme emphasis was on language and the way it was spoken and interpreted.

The great epic poem by Adam Mickiewicz, *Pan Tadeusz*, was on the program; it was the supreme expression of Polish Romanticism. Readers unfamiliar with it should imagine something like the *Iliad* or Tasso's *Jerusalem Liberated*. When Mickiewicz had begun to write it, Poland was still enslaved; and he said he considered his work an island to which he could flee, "closing the door on the noises of Europe."

Now, on that evening, the "noises of Europe," of a Europe shaken by war, burst deafeningly into the clandestine theater on the left bank of the Vistula River.

The performance went on—it was brisk and passionate, and the actors could lay claim to part of the credit. They were all magnificent; they all entered into their characters so commendably that they could inscribe them into the minds of the spectators. Halina, who had also been Karol's companion in the Wadowice recitals, was splendid; as were the new actresses, Danuta and Krystyna. Young Wojtyla was splendid, too, with his perfect diction and the crackling tension of his delivery.

From the street outside suddenly came the booming, imperious, intimidating sound of a loudspeaker. The military vehicle had stopped right under their window. "Wehrmacht headquarters announces that German armed forces are about to enter the city of Moscow."

It was just propaganda. The Nazi strategy consisted precisely of that very thing: to make people think the Germans were invincible. Then they would strike down their adversaries, not just physically but psychologically, to inspire fear and create a continual atmosphere of threat and terror.

In the living room, the spectators felt an electric shock; but it wasn't fright. From the time they arrived in this place they were well aware of the risk. All of this, however, lasted only an instant, an imperceptible split second, at the most, because the actor never hesitated or made the slightest pause.

Karol went on reciting, as if nothing had happened, not even speeding up the rhythm of the poetry. He went forward,

up to the call to battle that *Pan Tadeusz* breaks into at its conclusion: "It is war, war for Poland that we must fight, my brothers!"

At that point, both actors and spectators realized what had
happened—and not just symbolically, not just in the days of
Mickiewicz. Their Poland, too, the Poland occupied by the Nazis,
had not surrendered to the new oppressor. It had resisted, it had
reacted with courage to defend its memory, its culture, and hence
its own national identity.

That was what Karol felt in his mind, and what, moreover,
he had committed himself to doing every day—as a Pole, and as
a patriot.

When he had moved from Wadowice to Cracow, he had
immediately gone back to doing theater. He was well known
around town in artistic circles; he had entered an experimental
group and performed readings with them. The final performance
had been a work by Nizynski, *The Knight of the Moon*, a fairy
tale inspired by the zodiac. He had played the part of Taurus.
But three months later the Nazis had invaded Poland; and one
of the first decisions by the governor general had been to ban
all artistic and literary activity. The reaction of the Poles had
been immediate. From historical experience, they all knew that
the death of their culture automatically meant their own ex-
tinction as well. So various initiatives had sprung up, all of them,
naturally, in secret.

Theater groups were born, such as Studio 39, the best known
of them. Courses were set up for pupils in the upper middle
schools as well as for the students of the Jagellonian University.
These were held in private houses, often at night. Once the Gestapo had arrived unexpectedly at the Kydrynskis; but Juliusz's
mother was exceptionally adept, and she managed to make the
Germans believe that the circle of chairs they had set up was for
a family celebration.

Karol was very active; he was everywhere; and he wound
up joining *Unia*, the "Union." This was a clandestine Christian

organization that worked both in anti-Nazi resistance and planning for a new civil society, a new future state.

The movement had various sections. There was a military component, which managed to gather some twenty thousand men. There was a Council for Assistance to the Jews, which issued false identification papers, hid children, and gave financial help to the most indigent. There was also a group dedicated to cultural opposition, precisely because defending the written word and safeguarding language constituted a struggle for freedom, for the independence of the nation.

All those who entered *Unia* had to swear a solemn oath of loyalty; Karol did so, fully identifying with those ideals and with that particular kind of "combat." He had always been a quiet and peaceful person, non-violent we would say nowadays. Armed struggle was the furthest thing from his way of life, from his thinking, and, obviously, from the religious faith that he professed.

Like his contemporaries, Karol completed his military service, and one day he had to shoulder a rifle. Someone snapped his picture, and, many years later, showed it to him. Wojtyla noted with a grimace: "Fortunately, that was the only time...." The only time, that is, that he had ever held a weapon, and then only because he had been forced to do so.

For this reason, unlike many of his friends, he had not entered the armed groups that were engaged in sabotage or in fighting in the underground army, *Armia Krajowa*. Karol understood perfectly why people made such choices, and he respected them. For him, however, the "weapons" to be used for defending freedom were different. As his favorite poet Norwid had said: "I persist in thinking that the insurrection of the sword must be accompanied by the insurrection of thought."

Later, as Karol's commitment deepened, this attitude found an active and original outlet. He had help; because, in the meantime, his friend, the director, had arrived.

After the Germans had requisitioned his apartment,

Mieczyslaw Kotlarczyk had fortuitously managed to leave
Wadowice with his family to arrive in Cracow. Karol put him
up in his house. They took up the thread of the discussions
about theatrical experiments that they previously had spoken
about for many years. They finally managed to achieve
Kotlarczyk's old ideal of a *"rhapsodic theater,"* that is, a theater of the inner depths, of the living word, where rather than
simply watch the spectacle, one listened to it; and above all, a
theater that would once again present, in their essence, the cultural traditions of Poland.

So this was not just a new artistic genre, but a new form of
struggle, just as the founders of *Unia* had argued. For this reason, commitment to the theater, too, would no longer be an end
unto itself but would become a genuine instrument for resisting
Nazism. "It is a protest," Kotlarczyk said, "against the extermination of Polish culture on its very own soil."

The director, the stage designer, and the actors met twice a
week, on Wednesdays and Saturdays, before curfew, in Wojtyla's
apartment, which they called "the catacomb." The basement
flat was cold and dark; sometimes the power went out, and
they had to continue the rehearsals by candlelight. When they
left, they went one by one, taking a thousand precautions so as
not to attract any attention. They seemed to be conspirators; and,
perhaps, considering what they had in view, they really were.

The streets all around Tyriecka were blanketed with post-
ers that carried the ever-growing list of persons—often acquaintances or even friends—who had been sentenced to be shot.

They began the performances. The first one was held in the
Szkockis's villa. Then gradually they moved on to other private
apartments, but never the same one twice. The texts, which were
patriotic and sometimes religious too, were by the greatest ro-
mantic writers and poets, from Slowacki to Mickiewicz, like
Pan Tadeusz, which had been performed on that famous evening
when the Germans announced that Moscow would be captured
in a couple of days. But that capture never took place.

Hitler had wasted too much time on the southern front. He wanted to invade Ukraine and the Crimea first, because he was drawn to the enormous granaries and oil fields that stretched beyond the Caucasus. Even though Kiev had fallen, even though 650 thousand Russian soldiers had been taken prisoner, it had proved to be a huge strategic mistake.

In fact, when the Führer gave the order to aim for Moscow, it was already too late. Halfway through October 1941, the terrible autumn rains had begun; and so had the *rasputitza*, the muddy season that turned the roads into swamps. Then came the snowstorms, the winter, and the cold.

The German troops were forced to slow down, and then to stop. They had to abandon Rostow, suffering their first serious defeat. Nonetheless, the march toward Moscow continued. On December 2, a reconnaissance battalion reached Khimki, a suburb of the capital. From there, they could see the spires of the Kremlin.

Now, it seemed, they had done it. It was all over. But instead, four days later, General Zhukov sent a hundred divisions into the field. The Soviet attack was so unexpected, so tactically well prepared, and so decisive that the army of the Third Reich, forced to retreat, came out of the battle devastated and in ruin. But most of all—and this was the most important feature, on the psychological rather than the military level, on the level of morale—the myth of German invincibility had collapsed.

The same thing happened that evening on the left bank of the Vistula River in a little clandestine theater, where one could breathe in a little freedom and take courage again to resist the oppressor. It took tremendous energy to go on doing it. All around lay frightful desolation, and people continued to die or disappear in silence, never to be heard from again.

Kotlarczyk told Karol horrible news about his high-school classmates and about Wadowice. Silkowksi, his dearest friend, had been interned in a prison camp near Magdeburg. The other athletic classmate, Kesek, had been murdered, just like his two brothers. The synagogue had been blown up with sticks of dynamite.

The Nazis, the director told him, had forced a group of civilians to help with the explosion. They were poor women dressed in black, old men terrorized by being dragged from their houses. The SS captain had looked them over, one by one, with a grim expression. Before lighting the fuse, he had shouted: "So, now you'll see how these Jews get treated!"

The synagogue was near the school. The Wojtyla family had gone there a few times to hear Moishe Savitski sing. He was a young recruit from the Twelfth Infantry Regiment who had a marvelous voice.

Karol suddenly thought of his Jewish friend, Jerzy Kluger. "And the others?" he asked. Kotlarczyk couldn't tell him. "Nothing," he said, "nothing's known about them. It is as if they vanished."

It was a scene that, at times, had something incredible and surreal about it. On one side of the boiler department were stacked bags of phosphorus salts and sodium; on the other, the pails used to transport the chemical products. In the center, like boxers in the ring, stood the two of them, Karol and Mankowski, debating the existence of God, religion, the Church, and priests. In the end, somehow or other, they always managed to find a little common ground.

Chapter Eight

THE TAILOR-CATECHIST

To the boys who judged by their own standards, any man like that one, who was forty years old, with his hair gone gray, was an old fogy. He also spoke an odd sort of devotional language, old-fashioned, like a catechism. He had a vision of life that, at the time, seemed inconceivable. He also was a comic character, with his timid manner, his toothbrush moustache, and his extremely soigné style of dressing, as if he polished himself every morning.

Jan Tyranowski certainly didn't make a good impression on the lads. Or at least not during those first encounters in the parish church of Saint Stanislas Kostka, which Wojtyla also attended. Jan had a singular story. After studying engineering and being an accountant for a while, he suddenly dropped everything: he went to work in his father's tailor shop; that way, he said, he would have more time to dedicate to the parish, to the youngsters.

At first, Karol also thought he seemed to be over the hill, not the right sort of person to convey the ideals of the Christian faith and, above all, to translate them into simple, comprehensible language, and something that sounded like real life to boys. However, it wasn't long before he had to change his mind. Besides, it was just enough to look at Jan's bright blue eyes, with

their incredible magnetism, to realize that he had great cha-
risma.

In fact, he didn't have a hard time winning over the group
of teenagers either, overcoming their resistance and reserve. He
didn't give sermons or lectures; he "worked," so to speak, on
their souls. He thought their souls had to re-assimilate the truths
of the faith that they had learned from the catechism, so they
could finally arrive—without passing through a web of prohi-
bitions and restrictions—at a fuller interior life.

The God that Jan showed them—bearing witness with his
words and his conduct—was not the God of theological dis-
courses or books by priests. Instead, he was a God with whom
a person could live day by day, but he happened to be the God
of which they were not yet aware. Jan was always repeating a
phrase he had heard years ago from a priest friend: "It's not
hard to be a saint." It was as if to say that in the Church, holi-
ness shouldn't be the exclusive property of a small coterie of the
elect, of privileged and preselected individuals, but was funda-
mentally a vocation for everyone, a door open to the whole
world.

After the death of his father, Karol began seeing Tyranowski
more and more often. He took long walks with him along the
banks of the Vistula. He was seeking comfort for his pain, because, even though he prayed continually, even obstinately, he
couldn't forget that tragic moment. Along with softening his
grief, Jan, who was a man naturally given to contemplation,
helped Karol to deepen the experience of prayer by introducing
him to Carmelite mysticism, in particular to Saint John of the
Cross and Saint Teresa of Ávila.

Jan told him: "God is within us, but not because we've
trapped him inside the narrow limits of our human mind; God
is in us to draw us out of ourselves toward the place of his
supernatural transcendence."

One afternoon, the Nazis swooped down like furies on the
Debniki district and, without explanation, arrested the Salesian

priests who were in charge of the parish. All but two of the religious were deported to a concentration camp and never seen again.

At that point, there was a danger that all the parish's activities would come to a halt, and the place would close for good. Someone had the idea of turning to the lay people to ask for their cooperation. Tyranowski was given the charge of supervising the pastoral care of young people. He created the Living Rosary, a sort of fellowship with four leaders—one of whom was Karol—who looked after some sixty boys and young men ranging in age from fourteen to twenty-five years.

It was a fine effort, but a complicated one as well. It was also hard to manage because it had to operate in secret. Some of the young people got restless; they said they couldn't just stand by talking about religion while Poland was being massacred; and a few of them disappeared, going off to fight.

Whether they knew something or not, the Gestapo invaded Tyanowski's apartment; but he did a fine job explaining things and justifying the presence of all those boys. The Germans left, but clearly they would be back as soon as possible to investigate and recheck the premises. Those were the days of the roundups; and Juliusz Kydrynski was one of those arrested and deported to a concentration camp.

Jan advised Karol not to let himself be seen with the teenagers for a while, or at least not to have everyone meeting together. It was better to be prudent. Karol reluctantly agreed; he would miss those long conversations, the spontaneity, the naturalness, with which his friend had brought him a new approach to the faith and, hence, to a new way of thinking about and confronting life.

By way of compensation, Karol began to devour the books that Jan had given him, especially in the factory, sitting by the boiler, in the breaks at work. He borrowed a work authored by Saint John of the Cross, *The Dark Night of the Soul*. There was one passage which he never grew tired of rereading:

> I had no light or guide
> But the one that burned in my heart.
> It guided me safely
> And it surpassed the noonday sun....

He interpreted this "dark night" as the moment of suffering by the human soul when it is besieged by the luminous, purifying darkness of faith. In the end, that darkness allows the person to grasp their true dignity, the authentic meaning of his or her own freedom.

At first, Karol had been thunderstruck to discover the interior life and contemplative prayer. He thought of becoming a Carmelite monk; but the idea passed, or at any rate, the course of events drove it away. Nonetheless, his future vocation would reveal the crucial influence of those readings and that mystical experience. They would shape the synthesis of contemplation and the active life that would leave a profound imprint on both his human and spiritual adventure.

It was Jan who suggested another book, this one by the theologian Saint Louis Grignion de Montfort, that prompted Karol to reexamine his devotion to Mary, to check whether it hadn't turned into simpleminded religiosity or even sanctimoniousness.

Thus, he managed to reawaken his piety, to live it in a more mature, intense manner, a manner more embodied in the history of his time, the history of Poland, as he would do later when he went to the sanctuary of the Black Madonna in Częstochowa. In her presence, as he said, one could feel how the heart of the nation "was beating"; one could understand its problems, its worries, and its hopes.

Day after day, the moment for the definitive choice was approaching, the moment of truth, the truth of his life. It was unusual that Karol reached that moment primarily with the help of two laymen.

To be sure, Don Figlewicz, who was his confessor and spiritual father, had played a fundamental role. He had served as a companion all through those years on the long path of his quest. Archbishop Sapieha, together with the rector and the professors of the seminary that he would attend, had also played an important part in the story.

Nevertheless, it had first been a layman, his father, who had brought him to really "know" God. Then it was another lay person, Jan Tyranowski, who made him "see" God within himself. Still more than this, it had been the encounter with the timid tailor-catechist that left the deepest imprint upon his life and faith. That was probably why Karol would always have a rather unclerical view of the Church, of its structures and mission, as well as of the priestly ministry, the relationship between lay people and priests, and of the role of the laity in the Christian community.

Yet, he still had to take the final step. Here, at this point, Karol felt inspired and strengthened by an extraordinary Polish figure.

Adam Chmielowski had first been a great patriot: at only seventeen years of age he had taken part in the uprising of January 1863. He had been gravely wounded and had to have a leg amputated without anesthesia. He later studied painting and become a famous artist. In the end, however, he abandoned it all. He entered the Third Order of the Franciscans with the name of Brother Albert, dedicating himself to the service of the very poor and the handicapped.

Karol was fascinated by this character. Thanks to him, Karol understood how it could be possible, at a certain point in life, to cast aside even the dearest of things, such as art and literary interests, to answer the call that exploded within you. Then there was one particular feature of this man that had profoundly moved him: the "heroic" dimension in which Chmielowski had always viewed and carried out his mission, both in defending his homeland and in caring for the most abandoned people in society.

Karol thought the same way. He thought that a person always had to be ready, as we read in the Gospel, to "give up one's soul," one's very life.

At that crucial point in history, with all that was going on in the world, one might well ask oneself—as Elie Wiesel did after going through the dreadful experience of the Nazi death camps: Why is God so silent? Why doesn't he intervene? Why does he permit all this horror? In those years, just choosing God, or merely believing that God existed, became a true act of courage and heroism.

On Sunday morning, December 7, 1941, approximately four hundred Japanese planes, in two successive waves, attacked the airbase at Pearl Harbor, destroying or gravely damaging a considerable part of the United States' Pacific fleet. Of the ninety-six ships lying at anchor, eighteen were knocked out, beginning with the battleship *Oklahoma*, along with two hundred fighters and bombers. It was a real disaster for the American Navy, which would spend months recovering from the sudden losses.

The attack took not only the United States by surprise, showing its leaders just how unprepared they were, but Germany as well. For some time, Hitler had been asking the Japanese government to strike the Soviet Union in the back, perhaps in Vladivostock or Siberia. Most of all, he had warned against having "accidents" with the Americans. It was better to keep them out of the melee for a few months more, at least until Operation Barbarossa had made sufficient progress.

Instead, Japan, which was looking to control all of southeast Asia, rushed ahead to seize naval supremacy in the Pacific, as well as in the Indian Ocean and the Sea of China. So, to advance its own interests, it made what was militarily the most sensational and strategically the most harmful choice. That way, it obliged a reluctant Hitler to keep the promise he had made, and hence, to declare war on the United States of America. Even worse, this declaration literally dragged the United States out of its neutrality.

Now the Nazi regime would have to fight on another front and struggle with an extremely powerful adversary—as if it didn't already have enough troubles!

On the plains of Russia, mainly due to the tremendous winter cold and the attacks of the Soviet troops, Germany alone had lost a million men—who were either dead, wounded, or missing in action— not counting the losses of Italians, Hungarians, and Romanians.

The German soldiers were demoralized, hanging at the very end of their tether. Still, the leadership had to think about recruiting fresh forces as soon as possible. Of the one hundred sixty-two divisions drawn up in eastern Europe, only eight were in good enough condition to be used to attack. Meanwhile, instead of an invasion on Great Britain by Nazi troops, the cities of Germany were enduring horrific damage under the continual carpet bombings of the British Air Force.

Despite all this, Hitler continued to insist fanatically on the absurd and inhuman idea of not allowing the army to make a timely retreat; it had to hold, at any and all cost, the positions it had captured.

The war had definitely become a worldwide conflict. The human race seemed to have gone crazy, the victim of a collective sense of madness. It seemed to have given up all hope and accepted, as inevitable, the prospect of universal self-destruction.

Chapter Nine

"I WANT TO BECOME A PRIEST"

For some time now, Karol had already made his decision; but he kept thinking about it, all throughout the day and night. He even kept thinking about it at the factory, in the water purification department, for all he had to do was keep an eye on the boiler. And so, for the umpteenth time, Karol reviewed the beginning of the path that had led him to choose to become a priest.

It was only now, however, that he could say with absolute certainty that it hadn't been an unforeseen choice. It was not a recent one, or one tied in with the death of his father. Rather, it was the final, conclusive act of a long spiritual journey. As it happens with all religious to some extent, his vocation had its own particular evolution. It had matured through the most varied trials and experiences. It followed a trajectory that had, in part, been laid out by certain persons, environmental factors, and circumstances. Yet that decision, when all was said and done, he had been taken all by himself—up to the point, as he himself said, of the "inner illumination."

Every moment of his life had been like a brick that had served, as one was stacked on top of another, to build up to this vocation: his family, of course, his studies, his friendships, the theater, his work, his spiritual studies, and then the fact that he had been left alone so soon. Then, too, to be sure, there was the barbarity of the war, which had made him intuit the existence of a very close link between the priestly ministry and the defense of the dignity of the human person.

He heard the bell sound which meant his shift was over. Strange, but he didn't actually realize that the time had passed so quickly. He left the Solvay plant without changing clothes. He wore a shirt that was now threadbare, gray socks, and wooden clogs on his feet. That autumn, the autumn of 1942, had begun with bitterly cold temperatures, especially in the early morning. However, he didn't pay any attention to that; he hadn't even noticed the cold.

He stopped at the parish church of Podgorze, which was run by the Redemptorist Fathers, to attend Mass. He always went there, once the night shift was over, to find the strength to face another hard day. For that reason, he couldn't fail to keep going, on that day of all days—a special day, or one that ought to be.

He made his way toward the center of Cracow, hastening his stride as he went. He had hardly turned the corner when he ran into an SS patrol stationed across the street. During that time, they had orders to stop and question everyone; but the young worker looked too innocent, too unassuming, and too scruffy. The soldiers knew where he was coming from; and they thought that he was just in a hurry to dive into bed and get to sleep as soon as possible.

Crossing the marketplace square, which was all but deserted at that hour, Karol arrived in front of the great eighteenth-century palace, the residence of Archbishop Adam Stefan Sapieha. Everyone called him the "Prince," because of his aristocratic pedigree, but also because of the patriotism and courage he showed during the First World War and now was showing under the Nazi occupation. He maintained contact with resistance groups, with *Unia*, took care of the Jews and prisoners of war, and systematically turned down the ambiguous proposals for collaboration tendered by the governor general.

A truly great man! He had known how to uphold the honor of the nation and show his own dignity vis-à-vis everyone, un-like—some critics argue—the primate, Cardinal Augustyn Hlond.

People had never really forgotten some of Hlond's highly debatable remarks about the Jews, made just at the time when anti-Semitism was raging. In particular, they had not forgotten that Hlond had once declared: "It is a fact that Jews are fight-ing against the Church." Nor had they pardoned the way the cardinal, along with members of the government, had fled as the German troops were about to occupy Warsaw.

Karol recalled very well the day when he had first met Bishop Sapieha; although he felt a certain embarrassment whenever he relived the scene that took place some four years before in Wadowice.

After administering confirmation in the parish church, the archbishop had gone to the boys' high school. There, Wojtyla had been chosen, since he was the best student, to deliver a welcome address. Struck by the young man's eloquence and his elegant Latin, Sapieha had asked the religion teacher: "What is this student thinking of doing after he graduates?" To which the priest replied: "I don't think he's decided yet."

Karol was two steps away. Somewhat cheekily, he came for-ward. "Your Excellency, if you'll allow me, I can tell you my-self." After a sign of encouragement from the archbishop, he had explained: "I'm going to register at the Jagellonian Univer-sity to study Polish philology." "Too bad," Sapieha remarked with displeasure. "Too bad you won't be doing theology." Think-ing back to that story, Karol told himself, the archbishop had been right after all.

Meanwhile, he had arrived at 3 Franciszkanska Street. He knocked at the dark black gate; and when the nun answered, he told her the purpose of his visit. He immediately got the impression that the sister already knew something; quite probably, Don Figlewicz had arrived there first.

He climbed the big staircase, crossed several rooms, and felt the emotion well up inside him. All his boldness seemed to have evaporated. When he found himself face to face with the rector of the seminary, he was dismayed for a moment and couldn't get a word out. He took a deep breath and, resolute this time, said: "I want to become a priest."

By way of an answer, the rector smiled at him: he was accepted. Karol had already made secret visits to the seminary, studying there during his free time and presenting himself to the professors for exams. At the same time, so as not to awaken suspicion, he had to continue his everyday life and behave as usual.

The Germans had ordered the closing of all seminaries, peremptorily forbidding the admission of new candidates. Archbishop Sapieha had tried to dodge the ban by making arrangements for the would-be priests in the parish churches; but some had been discovered and arrested, and one had even been shot. Then the archbishop, without further delay, decided to create a clandestine seminary in his own palace.

Karol was not supposed to breathe a word of this to anyone; only later would he confide the news to his theater companions. He did so one evening, during rehearsals, hoping that the business could be dispatched quickly. Instead, without bothering about the curfew and the risks they were running, they burst into an animated discussion that lasted till morning.

Needless to say, the others were completely opposed. Halina was shocked when she heard the news. Even back in the Wadowice days, she knew about his deep piety and devotion; but precisely because he had shown other interests and hadn't entered a seminary after graduating from the *gymnasium*, she was convinced that he wouldn't become a priest and would go on performing as an actor.

Kotlarczyk, as a man of the theater, was extremely critical

and hostile. At first, he thought Karol wanted to become a monk. "Do you think you can solve everything by locking yourself up in a monastery?" He told Karol he was making a mistake, that his true vocation was the theater; there, and nowhere else, would he be able to serve God and Poland in the best way possible.

Then Tadeusz Kudlinksi, founder of the group *Studio 39*, took a shot at it. Taking advantage of the fact that Wojtyla had been his friend ever since his first days in the theater in Cracow, he tried a series of arguments that might be described as extortionate.

He began by citing, no less, the Gospel parable of the talents, paraphrasing it, and naturally, adapting it for his own purposes. He said that God had given Karol great gifts as an actor; and so, if he didn't cultivate and develop them, he wouldn't be bringing to fruition the talents he had received; and he wouldn't be able to return them when called to account.

Then Kudlinksi pulled his lowest trick, the one guaranteed to work. He reminded his friend of his favorite poet, Norwid: "What did he write in the *Promethidion*, borrowing from the Gospel of Luke? He wrote that, 'The light was not meant to be kept under a bushel.'" And what are you thinking of doing now? The exact opposite?"

However, Karol was unmovable. One by one, he refuted all of the objections. "The day comes," he said, "when, in the existence of a man, his destiny gets fulfilled. Now this has happened to me. I've been chosen, I can't say no. I can't reject this gift."

So a new chapter of Karol's life began; and it brought some extra difficulties with it because of all the precautions that he now had to take. Practically speaking, the only thing he could do openly, in the light of day, was to go on working at Solvay. Otherwise, on every occasion he had to behave with the greatest reserve and caution, for example, during the rehearsals in his apartment or performances in private homes, and now with the courses he was taking at the faculty of theology.

Karol and the other six seminarians could get together only from time to time in the archbishop's residence with their professors. Mostly, he studied by himself, poring over a book he had been given entitled *Metaphysics*. It was written in a difficult language, and so dry as to seem completely abstruse; but it was essential for getting into the spirit of scholastic philosophy.

It was frustrating for any young man, and for Karol in particular, to live that way: a buried, always secret, life. However, the situation itself made that clandestine behavior necessary: it was a direct consequence of what was happening then on the various German fronts. From the news reports coming in, a picture was now emerging that substantially reversed the one that had taken shape between the spring and the summer of 1942.

In Africa, the Germans had recouped their losses in the desert. Rommel's men had retaken Tobruk from the British. By the end of June, they had reached El Alamein, ready now to plunge toward the Nile Delta and conquer Egypt. Some crazy music-loving strategist had baptized it *"Operation Aida."*

Yet, Hitler was paying little heed to the African campaign. He sent Rommel an appointment as Field Marshal, but no reinforcements and no supplies. So, in early November, the Eighth British Army, under General Montgomery, was able to counterattack and break through German lines in the southern sector. The Führer's orders to "hold fast" and "not to retreat a step" only helped to worsen the defeat of the Italian-German forces.

A few days later, the Allies disembarked in North Africa. At 1:30 A.M. on November 8, American and British troops, under the command of General Dwight Eisenhower, landed on the coast of Morocco and Algeria.

The worst news, however, was from Russia. There, too, after the Reich's success in the summer along the Volga, in the Caucasus and in Maikop, famed for its oil deposits, the fortunes of war had sharply shifted.

Operation Barbarossa, which was supposed to lead to the

annihilation of the Soviet Union, was turning—exactly as had happened to Napoleon one hundred thirty years before—into a tragic failure. The conclusion of the dramatic battle around Stalingrad—even though the Germans had already occupied a good 90 percent of the city—only confirmed this once and for all.

On November 19, 1942, deploying more than a million men, and taking advantage of the early winter, the Soviets unleashed a powerful counteroffensive on the Don River in the middle of a snowstorm. General Paulus, the commander of the Sixth Army, made a desperate attempt to fight back, but it was all in vain.

At that point, Paulus sent a radio message to Hitler: "Further resistance is pointless. The army requests immediate authorization to surrender." Once again, Berlin dispatched a madman's reply: "I forbid the surrender. The Sixth Army will hold its positions till the last man and the last bullet."

With the new year, however, the surrender finally did occur. On the afternoon of February 2, 1943, a Luftwaffe reconnaissance plane flew over the city and reported by radio: "No sign of combat in Stalingrad." That same day, late in the morning, 91 thousand German soldiers—of the 285 thousand who had once made up that great army—had set off, along with their twenty-four generals, on a march to the prison camps of Siberia. Only five thousand of them would ever see their homeland again.

After Stalingrad, the downturn in German fortunes had an immediate repercussion on Poland: the repression was ratcheted up to an excruciatingly new level. Among those arrested was Tadeusz Kwiatkowski, a writer who was the fiancé of Halina. His friends also finally learned what had become of Juliusz Kydrynksi: he had been deported to a camp not far from Cracow called Oswiecim. At that moment, only a few Poles already knew that Oswiecim had changed its name, and now had a German one: Auschwitz.

Previous page: Karol Wojtyla sometime during the first year of his life. CNS

Left: Emilia Wojtyla with her son Karol Józef Wojtyla around 1920. CNS

Bottom: The Wojtylas, Emilia and Karol Senior, with Karol's older brother, Edmund. Karol's older sister, Olga, died as a tiny infant. Skapska

Karol Wojtyla as a young boy in a portrait with his father, Karol Wojtyla, Senior, in his army uniform. CNS

Twelve-year-old Karol Wojtyla (upper left) is pictured with his classmates at his parish school in Wadowice, Poland. CNS

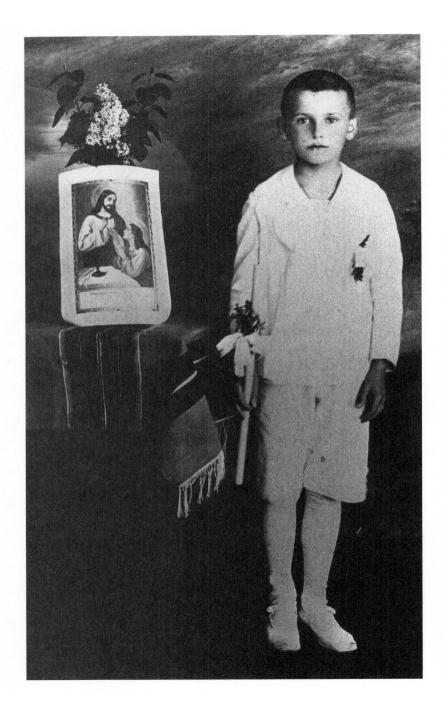

Previous page: Dressed in the traditional white suit, the future pope made his First Holy Communion in 1927. CNS

Left: Karol Wojtyla as a high-school student in Wadowice around 1938. CNS

Bottom: Father Karol Wojtyla poses with a group of children. Karol was ordained a priest on November 1, 1946. CNS

Top: Karol Wojtyla stands beside bikes on a cycling trip. An avid skier, cyclist, kayaker, and trekker, Karol never gave up his love of the outdoors. CNS

Right: This undated photograph shows Karol Wojtyla as a priest. CNS

As part of his pastoral work, Father Wojtyla led groups of students on excursions which included Mass, serious philosophical discussions, singing, joking, and fireside conversations. Wojtyla wore sports clothes in order to avoid being recognized by the police who could have arrested him for celebrating Mass in a forest. Skapska

Left: Always a fan of the outdoor life, Karol Wojtyla pauses for food on a camping trip. Skapska

Bottom: Combining his love for the outdoors with his scholarly pursuits, Karol Wojtyla takes time out from rowing his kayak to read—1955. CNS

Top: Bishop Karol Wojtyla walks among the ruins of the Parthenon temple in Athens, Greece, in 1963. CNS

Left: In this undated photograph, Karol Wojtyla relaxes at a forest campsite. Skapska

Top: Father Wojtyla pauses during a mountain trek. Skapska

Right: Father Karol Wojtyla is consecrated auxiliary bishop of Krakow at the Cathedral of Wawel on September 28, 1958, at the age of 38. CNS

Chapter Ten

"THE GHETTO NO LONGER EXISTS"

From all over Europe, the long convoys of armored railway cars began to arrive in Poland. The Nazis combed every occupied country for its Jews and then jammed them, like animals, into the trains. The journey was grueling, days and days without food or water; and some people didn't survive. When they arrived, the oldest Jews, in particular, along with the women and children, were immediately led into dark red buildings, which belched out a strange ash-filled smoke.

The plan to exterminate the Jewish people had been unleashed. The new Europe, the Europe dominated by the German "race" had to be *judenrein*, free and clear of non-Aryans. The Slavic peoples were considered an inferior species, to be reduced to slavery; but the Jews were lower still, less than nothing.

The "Final Solution," although it had been secretly planned for some time now, had not been immediately set into motion. It's true that, at the beginning of the war, special squads called *Einsatzgruppen* had carried out ferocious massacres of Jews. Their task, in most cases, was to cleanse the conquered territories of the people they called "subhumans" or "impure." The

Germans herded them together, region by region, and then locked them in the ghettoes of the larger Polish cities.

There, the Jews lived in horrendous conditions. There was no need to set up the death camps: the Jews were already dying fast enough on their own.

In Warsaw, the old medieval ghetto had become an immense prison once the Nazis built a ten-foot wall around it. Where 160 thousand people had once lived, there were now around 600 thousand. There were fourteen or fifteen people living in a single room. The German soldiers amused themselves by using the children for target practice whenever one tried to slip out at night to find something to eat.

Nevertheless, precisely through its desperate will to survive, the community had been transformed into one great resistance movement—all in secret, of course. There were theaters, schools, and cultural centers. There was a synagogue and printing presses that put out newspapers. Even the *ZOB*, the Jewish Fighting Organization, had come into being.

In Cracow, the Jews had been closed up in a completely fenced-in ghetto, which was watched over day and night. Here, too, there were dozens of deaths every day. Those who were considered strong enough to do so went out every morning to work in the Plaszow camp. A thousand lucky ones (as shown in the Steven Spielberg film) ended up on the "list" of Oskar Schindler, a Sudeten-German businessman, who by putting them to work in his factory, did the great service of saving them from certain death.

Archbishop Sapieha repeatedly protested to Governor Frank about the inhuman conditions in the ghetto; but the only thing the archbishop could do to help was order his parish priests to issue baptismal certificates to Jews, especially for their children, in order to get them to a safe place in the event of an inspection.

Karol was distraught. He couldn't understand it. In Wadowice, where he was born, he had enjoyed friendly rela-tionships with many people from the Jewish community, begin-

ning with his classmates and playmates. Thanks to their habit
of living together day after day, he had been able to get a close
look at Judaism and begin to know it from within, on every
level, including religiously and spiritually.

Now right here in Poland, however, the Jews were going
through terrible times. The outside world claimed to know little
or nothing about this persecution. They closed their eyes to what
was actually happening in the concentration camps that were
now full of people, especially Jews.

It was not yet realized that Poland had been chosen inten-
tionally and in a premeditated manner by the Nazi leaders to be
the epicenter of the Final Solution. Poland already contained
three million of the ten million Jews living in Europe; so it would
be easier to hide those crimes in a country that was entirely
occupied, and partly annexed to the Third Reich.

So the death camps, the *Vernichtungslager*, had been installed in Treblinka, Majdanek, Belzhets, Sobibor, Wolzek, and,
of course, Auschwitz, the number one camp, at the center of a
highly developed web of communications. It had four enormous
gas chambers which used the murderous Zyklon B gas, and
crematory ovens capable of making six thousand persons disappear every day.

Everything was organized and ready. Then, the course of
the war, which was taking longer than expected, speeded up the
pace of the extermination. On January 20, 1942, in Wannsee, a
suburb of Berlin, the German party officials decided to proceed
with the Final Solution. The head of the Gestapo, Reinhard
Heydrich, set out the general principles; and, from that moment on, the Jewish "problem" was dealt with in a systematic
and deadly fashion.

It was precisely at this time that the deportations from the
occupied countries of Europe began. The "death trains" often
arrived at Birkenau, which was a part of Auschwitz; and the
first registered convoy, on March 26, 1942, came from Slovakia
with almost one thousand women aboard.

Then it was the turn of the Polish Jews and, in particular, of the Jews of Warsaw. The armored cars left full, twelve thousand persons at a time, and returned empty from Treblinka. There was no way out. The solutions for escaping that torment became more and more desperate. In the hospitals, nurses broke the legs of old people so that they couldn't be transported, or injected them with morphine. One young pediatrician, Adina Blady Szwajger, had given cyanide to her little patients to spare them the horror of the gas chambers.

Nonetheless, thousands of Jews thronged the eastern rail station of *Ostbahnhof* every day. The Germans had thought up a diabolical, yet extremely simple, plan to convince the people to get on the trains: they offered each Jew three kilos of bread and one of marmalade. At that point, hunger was a thousand times stronger than fear.

The deportations from the capital had begun on July 22; by the end of September, almost three hundred thousand persons had been murdered.

This sort of butchery wasn't enough. A few days after the defeat at Stalingrad, Heinrich Himmler, the head of the SS, ordered the Warsaw ghetto to be destroyed. The operation— *Grossaktion*, as it was called—was entrusted to General Jürgen Stroop, who was the "right man" for that sort of thing. He assured his superiors that, in three days, he would put on board the trains the sixty thousand Jews who were still there.

At 6 A.M. on April 19, 1943, the first Nazi contingent entered the ghetto. The tanks drove in first to provide cover, then the artillery, the flamethrowers, and many squads of snipers.

At the intersection of Mila and Zamenhof Streets, a hail of shots and explosions came down from one of the buildings: rudimentary homemade Molotov cocktails, handmade grenades, and secretly purchased machine guns. The Germans were forced to retreat; they had already lost twelve men. A tank and two armored vehicles had been blown up, and some streets were completely mined.

The sons of David had not been content to mourn their evil fate; as they had not done for centuries, they showed that they knew how to fight, and reacted to violence and injustice. They had armed themselves and transformed the cellars, sewers, and basements of the ghetto into a whole series of little forts; and now they were fighting heroically against the enemy.

A very large number of them were young; there were also women who could shoot with both hands and who had bombs hidden beneath their dresses. All of them displayed incredible courage. Rather than end up as prisoners, they would rather die fighting, like Mordechai Anielewicz, the commander of the *ZOB*, who was only twenty-four years old at the time of his death.

Instead of three days, it took four weeks to overcome the resistance of the people whom Stroop's reports defined as "Jewish bandits" and "riffraff of an inferior race." The entire quarter—twenty-seven thousand houses in all—was leveled to the ground. In the sewers and cellars where they had taken refuge, many old people, women, and children were horribly burnt alive. And the seven thousand who survived—apart from the few who managed to escape—were taken directly to the gas chambers of Treblinka.

At 8:15 P.M. on May 16, SS Brigadeführer Jürgen Stroop commanded the synagogue to be torched. In his notary's style, he wrote the final dispatch to the governor general: "What was once the Jewish quarter of Warsaw no longer exists." Stroop then set himself to completing the official report, written on deluxe stationery, bound in leather, and richly illustrated.

Karol learned of the massacre. A few weeks later, he got direct information about the tragic liquidation of the Cracow ghetto.

He thought, with anguish, about Wadowice, about his Jewish companions and their families. It was most likely terrible for him to recall those faces, those persons, who had been part of his life.

He often went to the house of Jerzy Kluger, on the first floor of the large residence that looked out over the Rynek, the market square. He knew Jerzy's lawyer father well, his mother Rosalia, his old maternal grandmother, and his sister, the ever-so-gentle Tesia, blond and blue-eyed, who played tennis and was already a magnificent athlete. She must have turned twenty recently. How were they? Did they manage to escape?

Karol did not yet know that Kluger, the lawyer, and his son had tried to reach the Polish army. When they got to Lviv, they had fallen into the hands of the Russians and had been deported to Siberia, to a "re-education camp."

Nor did Karol know what had happened at Wadowice.

One day in July 1943, the SS "assistants"—Ukrainians, Latvians, Lithuanians, and some Polish collaborators—had entered the ghetto and forcibly ejected the frightened men and women. They huddled all of them together in Targowica Square, under a broiling sun, surrounding them with a hastily erected fence to prevent escape, just as they did on Thursdays at the livestock market. Meanwhile, other Jews continued to arrive from nearby towns, dragging behind them all their wretched worldly goods.

Now, there were more than a thousand of them. They looked at one another, still unable to grasp what they should have done, and where they would be going.

An SS officer approached a man dressed in black who had a violin case under his arm and yelled at him: "Play something, but make it catchy!" He had hardly begun when the others began shouting at him to stop. The man wound up putting the violin back in its case, and a soldier smacked him with the butt of his rifle.

Some individual was passing through the crowd collecting money and valuables, necklaces, bracelets, and earrings. One woman, who evidently knew him, had started railing against him: "Dirty traitor? Aren't you ashamed?" After tearing up some bank notes, she had thrown them in the collector's face. A soldier struck her repeatedly, and she collapsed on the ground in a pool of blood.

At that point, they were all lined up into columns, marched to the station, and put aboard the trains, as a loudspeaker droned: "Now you will be going to a work camp, where you will find food and lodging." On the door of one car there was a faded sign in chalk: "Auschwitz."

The passengers on that train included Kluger's mother and sister. His grandmother, ninety years old and practically blind, had been taken away some days before, and wound up in Belzhets, one of the largest death camps. Not one of the three women ever returned home.

Despite these events in Poland, the fortunes of war were looking more and more favorable for the Allies. With Operation Husky, the landing in Sicily had taken place in a strange atmosphere of competition between the British and the Americans. When Mussolini had been toppled and put under arrest, Hitler was beside himself. He was even more enraged by the armistice signed between Italy and the Western powers.

In the Atlantic, the German fleet was being routed, time after time, and the same thing was happening to the Luftwaffe in the skies of Europe. Half a million men had been used to try to stem the tide of battle with the Soviet Union, but that hadn't been enough. In fact, the Red Army had reconquered the line stretching from Orel to Kharkov, Smolensk, and Kiev, and had now arrived on the frontier of Poland and Romania. The worse the situation became for the Germans, the more their leaders seemed to want to vent their bestial instincts of revenge on the most defenseless and helpless people of all, the Jews.

Chapter Eleven

THE HEROES
OF MONTECASSINO

U p until that point, they had all failed: Americans, Indians, New Zealanders, and French colonial troops hadn't managed to conquer Montecassino. They hadn't yet succeeded in bringing down the "Gustav Line," as the Nazis called it. They couldn't even eject the Germans after the Benedictine monastery had been culpably bombed—the "useless destruction," it was called—by Allied Flying Fortresses.

Safe within their bunkers, which were dug out of the rock, the German soldiers hadn't had any problems repelling one enemy attack after another and maintaining complete control over that strategic crossroads.

After the landing at Anzio, the advance had turned out to be too slow and uncertain; the American bridgehead had been blocked. The German front had to be broken down from some other sector. Thus, in March 1944, the Allied commanders decided to take fresh aim at the Gustav Line. They proposed to General Wladyslaw Anders, the commander of the Second Polish Army Corps, that they take part with his men in the attack on Montecassino, "the impregnable Montecassino," as everyone now called it.

Anders had fled the massacre of Katyn and managed to organize this army, which primarily consisted of Poles who had been deported to Siberia following the Ribbentrop-Molotov pact, along with a million and a half of their compatriots. Only after the outbreak of hostilities between the Russia and Germany had they finally been allowed to leave the Soviet gulags, get military training in Iraq, and gather together in the Kresowa Fifth Division. Kresowa was derived from word *kres*, meaning "borders," in memory of the territories in eastern Poland occupied by the Red Army, to which they hoped to return one day and find liberated.

For this very reason, Anders and his fifty thousand men—joined by soldiers and officers who secretly left Poland and crossed Hungary—had accepted the daunting task of driving the Germans out of their fortifications at Montecassino. They wanted to show everyone that they were alive, that they existed. They wanted to fight for their own freedom and for the freedom of others: that had been the motto of the Polish legions ever since the Napoleonic wars.

If they won, if they succeeded in that desperate enterprise, they could lay claim, once the war was over, to fair "recognition" from the Allies. They could ask that their country's independence and national sovereignty be respected in the face of Moscow's hegemonic claims.

At that same time, in Cracow, Wojtyla was convalescing after a serious traffic accident. He had nearly lost his life. The fact that he had made it was due mainly to the timely intervention of a woman named Jozefa Florek.

It had happened on February 29. Late that afternoon, after finishing his shift at the Solvay factory, Karol was walking home. At a turn on Konopnicka Street, he had been run over by a military truck—the driver never saw him—and flung into a ditch. He didn't seem to be breathing, and blood was gushing from his head.

Florek, who was operating a tram, had seen him and

jumped down to help. She couldn't do it all by herself, so
she flagged down a car with a German officer aboard. Together, they had cleaned the blood off and realized that Karol
was still alive. A wooden lorry was passing by; the officer stopped
it and ordered the driver to take the young worker to the near-
est hospital.

The diagnosis was a concussion, a lesion on his shoulder,
and numerous wounds to the body. When he regained consciousness, some eighteen hours later, Karol found his head wrapped
in bandages and his arm in a plaster cast. He took the accident
philosophically. Indeed, he ended up seeing it as a providential
sign and a confirmation—since he had survived—that he had
made the right choice in deciding to become a priest.

When his long recuperation period ended towards the end
of April, he began going back to the seminary. He went there in
the morning and served the archbishop's Mass. There, he often
found Andrzey Zachuta, another clandestine seminarian whom
he had known in the days of the Living Rosary.

One day, Wojtyla found Zachuta missing. He rushed to his
house, where the neighbors told him that the Gestapo had
swooped down the night before and arrested Zachuta. They
had discovered that he was working in an organization that
helped the Jews: he tried to get baptismal certificates to save
them from deportation. Some days later his name appeared on
a list of those condemned to death, and Andrzey died in front
of a firing squad.

Karol was traumatized. So many of his friends were already
dead; and he didn't even know that five of his high-school classmates—Kluger, Czuprynski, Romanski, Bernas, and Kogler—
were fighting at Montecassino, the first two in the artillery, the
other three in the infantry.

On the night between May 11 and May 12, the Polish Army
Corps launched its offensive. To many people, including some
of Anders' own officers, it seemed almost suicidal to order an
operation like that, sending the soldiers out into the open with-

out a strong backup. It would have been better, they said, to go around the mountain and hit the Germans from behind. In fact, the attack did end in a real disaster; and the casualty lists were tragically long.

After a week, though, the criticism had already been forgotten; and the assault began all over again. All the able-bodied Poles were called on to fight, including men in the quartermaster corps and support services, drivers, mechanics, and cooks. At first light on May 18, 1944, the Third Karpati Division took hill 593. The only thing left was to climb to the monastery.

At 7:30, the order went out for the Twelfth Regiment of the Podolian Uhlans; and two hours later, a patrol spearheaded its way into the monastery. There were only twelve Germans waiting for them—sitting out in the open, unarmed, lost, driven almost insane by the tremendous, incredibly long siege. The others, desperate not to be taken prisoner by the Poles, whom they hated as much as the Russians, had fled toward the British on the western front; they risked being blown to pieces as they crossed the mine fields.

At 9:50 A.M. on the dot (for some reason all the official accounts would say 10:30), Second Lieutenant Gurbiel planted the red and white Polish flag on the rubble of the monastery. Immediately afterwards, the Union Jack was raised at Anders insistence, as a sign of the great joint effort by the entire Eighth Army, to which the Poles also belonged. Yet, for the record, the British didn't arrive at the abbey until four hours afterwards, as the Podolian Uhlans were already leaving.

However, it wasn't over. In reality, the battle of Montecassino—and this is a truth not always found in history books—ended seven days later. First, the entire German line of defense, the "Adolf Hitler Line," had to be demolished. It stretched from the slopes of Mount Cairo and the Piedmontese town of San Germano, to the Aquino airport, thereby blocking the passage of the Liri River valley.

Here, too, there were furious battles, with Anders' soldiers in the middle of it, in particular the Sixth Tank Regiment, and at the head of the Allied troops. In the end, they managed to break the Nazi resistance and occupy the Piedmont, which had been reduced to a pile of debris.

At that point, there were no obstacles left. The road to Rome lay wide open now, and the Poles would get to take it as conquerors. Instead, incredibly enough, an order arrived from headquarters to "rest." But were they really supposed to rest—or give way to others?

Without having sure proof, it's difficult to answer that question and thus attempt a historical reconstruction of those days. The fact remains, though, that it was the American forces under General Mark Wayne Clark, and not the Poles, who were the first to enter Rome as liberators.

In the same month of June, the Allies unleashed a stunning double attack. On D-day, Tuesday, June 6, the largest army ever seen opened the Anglo-American offensive on the western front with more than five thousand ships, thirteen thousand airplanes, and almost three million men. Their attack came as a surprise. The fleet arrived on the coast of Normandy, stunning the Germans, who were convinced that the invasion was not imminent, partly because of the stormy weather.

At dawn, on the stretch of ocean between the Vire River and the mouth of the Orne, Allied landing craft unloaded the first contingents of troops, under the cover of murderous fire. Shortly after midnight, three air transport divisions had already pounced down on the Seventh German army, and had already liberated the French village of Sainte-Mère-Église. (Those who have seen the film *The Longest Day* will recall the scene where a soldier named Steel parachutes down and gets entangled in the church's bell tower.)

For once, Hitler had possessed the correct intuition: the danger, he had insisted, would come from the direction of Normandy and not Calais. Then, once the Allied landing began, he lost an enormous amount of time waiting for events to unroll. He didn't give his first order until 4:55 in the afternoon; and it was, as usual, absurd beyond the limits of madness. It read: "The coast where the bridgehead is must be cleaned up by tonight at the latest." The Führer rudely silenced Rommel, who had proposed to pull the army back out of the range of enemy artillery.

In these same weeks, as France and Belgium were being liberated, the other attack started up; this time it came from the east. The Soviet troops first surrounded fifty German divisions in the Baltic regions. Then they wiped out the whole group of armies in the center, pressing all the way into Finland, which soon surrendered and revolted against the Nazis.

Thus, the Red Army overflowed into the central route, advancing four hundred miles in a few days, till it reached the Vistula, right in front of Warsaw. On the southern front, it conquered Romania, with the oil fields at Ploiesti, which was the only place the German armies could refuel, and finally forced Bulgaria to lay down its arms.

This was the crucial moment of the Second World War. It had been prepared by the conquest of Montecassino, the victory that opened the doors for the liberation, not only of Italy, but all of Europe. Much credit had to go to the heroism and sacrifice of Anders' men. As the English General Leese, the commander of the Eighth Army, had recognized, "The monastery of Cassino was taken by Polish units. It was truly a hard and exceptionally difficult battle. The effort by the Poles was great."

Two classmates of Wojtyla, Bernas and Romanski, the latter wounded three times, won the highest decoration of military honor. But what "treatment" would be reserved for those men and for their country?

At the Conference of Teheran, in September 1943 (that is, before Montecassino), Churchill and Roosevelt had bowed to the pressures of *Realpolitik*; or at least they failed to oppose Stalin and the increasingly self-important claims of the Russian dictator. By that time, the future of Poland and its eastern regions could already be described as compromised. After Teheran, things got even worse. The West would be the first to abandon the Polish people to a bitter destiny.

General Anders would significantly entitle his memoirs, *Without the Last Chapter*. Forty years, in fact, would have to pass before that chapter could be written. For Poland, they would be forty years of slavery.

Chapter Twelve

POLAND BETRAYED

Karol was just about to leave to join his friends, who were waiting for him on the Twardowski hills, for a little game of soccer. Just as he was about to open the door, he heard the sinister, unmistakable sound of the German high boots. The SS were reconnoitering the city, street by street.

They had arrived at the Debniki section, at Tyniecka Street, and must have already entered number ten by now. Their heavy steps grew closer.

At home with Karol were the Kotlarczyks, but at that very moment he was alone in the small entrance way. He was praying and he was afraid. He prayed stretched out on the ground, with his arms forming a cross, his heart in his mouth. He heard the shouts of the soldiers, who had climbed to the upper storeys. They were cursing the women who didn't want to part with their husbands, whom the Germans were dragging off.

When the SS came downstairs, Karol thought: "Now they'll go away." But they didn't. There was a sudden fearful silence. The young man understood and felt a shudder run down his spine. He realized that the soldiers had stopped in front of his door and were probably wondering if there was anybody in the basement.

It was Sunday, August 6, 1944, "Black Sunday" as it came

to be known. The governor general, Hans Frank, had given the word for this gigantic roundup. He ordered the arrest of all the men, and of any other person who might be in the least bit suspicious. Frank didn't want what had happened in Warsaw a few days before, where an uprising had broken out, to be repeated in Cracow.

In the capital, the Germans had issued a call-up for one hundred thousand men to work on the fortifications. It was only too clear that they planned to defend the city at any and all costs without paying the slightest attention to the very high risk they were running, not just of destroying Warsaw, but of causing enormous civilian casualties.

At that point, the Polish government was in exile and the leadership of the *Armia Krajowa,* that is, the clandestine army, had decided to attack the Germans because the Red Army was on the right bank of the Vistula River and already moving into the suburbs.

This operation had been given the name *Burza*, meaning "storm," which also happened to be the title of a poem by Norwid. The plan was very simple and straightforward. On the one hand, from within the city, the thirty thousand soldiers of the *Armia Krajowa* would go into action; on the other hand, from the outside, the Soviets would advance. The Nazis would be caught in the middle, and the fighting wouldn't last long. Human life and property would be spared, more or less as would happen three weeks later in Paris, which was quickly liberated with the help of American troops.

On August 1, at five o'clock in the afternoon, the assault had begun. The following is the report given by one of the protagonists, General Tadeusz Komorowski, the supreme commander of the insurgent forces:

From some windows, a hail of bullets rained down on the Germans who were passing through the streets, on their buildings, and on their marching formations. In the blink of an eye, civilians fired from streets. From the doors of the houses our men went off on the attack.

In the earliest phase, thanks to the surprise factor, the rebels managed to conquer two-thirds of Warsaw, including the entire center. However, it was a very precarious and provisory success; and strategic positions, such as the airport and the bridges on the Vistula, remained in Nazi hands.

After a few days, the Germans regained the upper hand by recapturing the western sectors; immediately they took reprisals, the first of a round of massacres. SS and police formations executed thirty-eight thousand persons, most of them civilians, and then many clandestine soldiers, the "bandits," as Hitler called them, as well as the wounded who couldn't leave their hospital beds.

The Poles had courageously gone on fighting and resisting, neighborhood by neighborhood, all the way to the cemeteries, and within the cathedral of Saint John, around the main altar. However, the disparity of power in men and, especially, in armaments was too great. The insurgents had only a thousand machine guns, pistols, and hand grenades, while the Nazis could count on the support of heavy artillery, tanks, as well as planes.

Then something happened that no one ever expected: suddenly and inexplicably, the help from the Soviets fell through. The Red Army stopped at the Vistula River, interrupting the offensive. There it stayed, just looking on, without intervening, without firing a shot.

There was more. The British squadrons that were trying to bring supplies to the Poles who were under siege were denied permission to land at the Russian bases. As a result, the planes had to take off from Brindisi and make a round trip of three thousand miles while dodging enemy artillery and fighter planes.

The Soviet air force could have carried out the same support operation with flights barely covering sixty miles.

Stalin had revealed his true intentions. He did *not* want a "free, strong, and independent" Poland, as he had so often proclaimed in the past, shamelessly lying. His answer to appeals from Churchill and Roosevelt had been incredibly hypocritical: he said that the USSR dissociated itself from the fate of Warsaw because the underground Polish army launched the insurrection without having a preliminary understanding with the Red Army. At least Marshall Konstanty Rokossowski, commander of the Byelorussian front, had been more sincere: he flatly declared that the Soviet army had to be the liberators of Poland and Warsaw, and not, he added verbatim, "the others," that is, the Poles.

Even more hypocritical, and yet more incredible, was the attitude of the western powers. In order not to irritate the Russian dictator, they had accepted his reply as valid. That way, they perpetrated a colossal betrayal of the Polish people, coldly sacrificing them on the negotiating table with Moscow to the new configuration of Europe.

Let us imagine, hypothetically, that the Warsaw uprising had succeeded. What would have happened? The Russians would have been welcomed as allies, although only as guests, in the capital of a nation that was independent, sovereign, and free. In that case, they would not have entered as conquerors, as the new bosses of the country.

Stalin, in other words, had played his cards right. By ordering the Soviet army not to intervene and to remain put on the Vistula, he had been able to achieve his objectives to have the Nazis themselves—paving the way for him—liquidate the Polish resistance. Otherwise, once the war was over, that resistance movement would have given rise to the leadership cadres of democratic parties. Then, too, he wanted the whole responsibility for the failure of the uprising to fall upon the Polish government in exile, to discredit it on the international level.

Thus, owing to the compliance of the Allies, Stalin had created all the prerequisites for concluding the "game" of the Polish question in his favor. Warsaw was now destined to be an almost imperceptible, and in any event, quite negligible, dot on the geopolitical map.

Although massacred and betrayed, Poland continued to cause fear, even for the Nazis. The Poles, with their desperate heroism, were a cause for concern. For this reason, preoccupied as he was with the notion that the capital would become a "hotbed," and that the chaos would then spread to the rest of the country, Governor General Frank had unleashed all the forces available for that police roundup in Cracow. On Black Sunday, more than eight thousand men and adolescents were arrested; and many of them wound up in concentration camps.

At 10 Tyniecka Street, the SS continued to look at one another indecisively, perplexed, as if to ask: was this basement inhabited? Behind the door, spread-eagle on the ground, Karol apprehended that silent questioning pause. It lasted just a moment, but it seemed an eternity. Finally, he heard the sound of the boots heading off: liberation! He was safe. He realized he was safe.

Archibishop Sapieha, seeing that the situation was worsening, decided to keep his seminarians tucked away in the archbishop's residence. He sent a priest over to Karol to inform him and take him to the palace on Franciszkanska Street. The military patrols were everywhere—every corner, around every intersection there could be a threat.

Mrs. Szkocka offered to accompany him. She went ahead first, to check that there were no dangers; and, behind her, Wojtyla and the priest, who hugged the walls of the houses and, at the slightest sign, ducked into the first available gateway. In such a fashion they crossed the entire city: a Cracow that was deserted, spectral, with its people shut up in their homes.

There was a soldier standing guard near the archbishop's residence; but fortunately he didn't notice them. As soon as he arrived, Karol, like the other seminarians, put on a cassock.

Thus, if the Germans burst in, they would have taken him for a cleric. Since he no longer went to the factory—and the SS were beginning to ask questions about the worker who hadn't signed the time card in a long while—Archbishop Sapieha arranged with the director of Solvay to have Wojtyla's name dropped from the list of active employees.

Meanwhile, the tragedy of Warsaw reached its climax. At one certain moment, there had actually been a glimmer of hope. The Red Army had finally moved. It had chased the Germans out of Praga, an outlying district on the east bank of the Vistula. Everyone thought that this new development might turn the uprising around. The leaders were already thinking of shelving their plans to surrender.

However, it was just an illusion. The Soviet army sank back into its profound lack of interest in what was happening on the other side of the river.

By contrast, the German commander retook the initiative. He brought in an armored division of the Wehrmacht and, in no time at all, recaptured the northern and southern sectors of the city. At that point, after sixty-three days of fighting, there was nothing more to do. The Polish authorities, both civilian and military, accepted the terms of capitulation proposed by the Nazis, provided the principles of the Geneva Convention were respected.

Almost two hundred thousand persons were dead, among them many women and children. Another fifty thousand were deported to concentration camps, and fifteen thousand were sent into forced labor in Germany. All the other inhabitants were forced to leave their homes before a terrifying cataclysm swept down on the capital.

Hitler had escaped an assassination attempt. He personally gave the order, disdaining the conditions that had been subscribed to, that the entire city was to be destroyed, literally leveled to the ground, house by house. Hitler supposedly made the horrific, criminal joke that nothing taller than two feet should be left standing. It would be, in fact, a mere phantom of War-saw, which is what the men of the Red Army saw a few months later when they occupied the capital.

Nothing was saved. Archives and libraries were burned. The walls of the cathedral were blown up, as were those of the Royal Castle and of many other buildings of artistic and architectural value. Even the statue of Christ the Savior with his cross, which had stood in front of the church on the Royal Road, ended up beneath the rubble, a symbol of tortured Poland.

Nevertheless, even though it had failed, the insurrection constituted a noteworthy event in Polish history. It was, so to speak, the culmination of five years of resistance and struggle by the entire nation against the oppressor. In the Europe occu-pied by Nazism, it was the only military action of such vast dimensions. In fact, as Himmler himself declared to the Ger-man generals, it was "the fiercest fighting since the beginning of the war, just as heavy going as the street fighting in Stalingrad."

Confined to the archbishop's residence, under "house arrest," as Karol called it, where, for better or worse, he was sheltered from the conflict. Karol lived through the drama of Warsaw in mental torment, but also with a sense of gratitude and admira-tion for those who were fighting in defense of the homeland, especially for those young men who had generously given their lives in the insurrection to save the freedom of everyone.

"I, too," he would say later, "belong to that generation; and I think that the heroism of the men and women who are my age has helped me to define my personal vocation."

Chapter Thirteen

THE FALSE LIBERATORS

The wait had been going on for many days now. The longer the wait became, the more it became spasmodic, dramatic, and full of anguish. It was evident that the Germans would go sooner or later. But when? When would they leave?

The first group, a large one, made up of civilians, had already fled Cracow. With them they had taken everything they could plunder—although there wasn't much left to plunder due to the systematic looting that Governor General Frank had carried out for years in the museums, libraries, and private homes.

The soldiers still remained in Cracow. The army had created a series of defensive posts; and the engineers had set up explosive charges at strategic points. There was a danger that the city could be chosen as the ultimate line of resistance, or that it might be destroyed as Warsaw was. When, oh when, would the Germans go?

People understood that the Third Reich had suffered a serious defeat. At that moment, though, they still didn't know that Hitler's counteroffensive, aiming to carry the war outside German territory, had failed, and that his attempt to break the lethal encirclement of Germany by the Allies on the east and west had likewise come to grief.

Everyone had been called up to serve, including workers, white-collar employees, and even old men. Young men at the universities and teenagers in high schools had also been raked in. The Führer had immediately thrown these half million recruits into the brawl, to crack through the western front in the French Forest of Ardennes. Just before Christmas, the battle to take the Bastogne, a crucially important junction in Belgium, had been furious. After some partial successes, however, the Germans had been driven back, suffering enormous losses.

On January 17, 1945, as he did every evening, the archbishop of Cracow was presiding over services in his chapel. Now, for several minutes, though, Archbishop Sapieha noticed that the priests and seminarians had been twitching with excitement; something was making them nervous and restless. After the Hail Marys, the Our Fathers, and the Glory Bes, a continual buzz kept surfacing. With every boom that came from outside, each louder and more nerve-racking than before, the looks they exchanged became more and more anxious.

"Is that the Germans?" they asked. "Or is it the others, the Russians, approaching?"

To tell the truth, not much was known about the Soviets either, only that the Red Army had remained stuck for weeks on the Vistula River and in eastern Prussia. That was all. If it hadn't been for their planes, which came to bomb the enemy positions, one might have thought that they had stopped fighting.

However, with the new year, Russia had unleashed its most massive offensive since the start of the war. Hitler was the only one who didn't believe it. When he was told, he exclaimed: "It's the greatest bluff since the days of Genghis Khan." Yet, what he considered a bluff was no fewer than one hundred eighty divisions.

Two Soviet armies had set their sights on Danzig. The armies commanded by Zhukov had conquered Warsaw and in a few days would get to within a hundred miles of Berlin. Konev's armies were aiming at Silesia, and Cracow was in the path of their advance.

The archbishop's chapel was suddenly shaken by a terrifying, shattering explosion. All of the windows in the building were blown to pieces by the violent displacement of air. The youngest seminarians, in particular, were terror-stricken. Stanislaw Starowieyski, who was standing next to Wojtyla, couldn't contain himself. "They've blown up the bridge," he shouted, "the Debniki Bridge."

Archbishop Sapieha sent the priests and seminarians to the cellar, where they would be safer. To make them forget their fear, he went back to reciting the rosary, deliberately raising his voice. But the fear wouldn't let go. Part of the problem was that down in the basement they were standing in the dark, the temperature was below freezing; and now there was an eerie silence, even more threatening than the terrifying explosions before it.

A little after midnight—it was now January 18—they heard a knocking at the gate. One of the priests went up to see who it was. It turned out to be Russian soldiers dressed like ragamuffins. They walked in a bit arrogantly, saying they had orders to check for any Nazis who might be hiding there. In fact, they were just looking for something to eat and drink, vodka if possible. They were exhausted. They could go on no longer after all that fighting and seeing all those deaths.

In the morning, a great celebration erupted. Everyone rushed out into the streets and city squares to show their joy. Even the seminarians, after their long, enforced seclusion, left the archbishop's residence to taste those first marvelous moments of freedom with the people.

The Debniki Bridge had been destroyed and was useless; but the frozen Vistula River could be crossed on foot. Karol ran to Tyniecka Street to embrace the Kotlarczyks and his other friends, Jan Tyranowski, Mr. and Mrs. Szkocki, and the Kydrynskis. Juliusz had already returned from the concentration camp.

Tadeusz Kwiatkowski had been liberated too; he and the actress Halina had decided to get married as soon as possible.

Everybody was crazed and intoxicated with joy; but they had to think about tomorrow. They had to build and lay down the foundations for a life that would finally be normal. The seminarians did their part. They repaired the damage to the archbishop's palace. They moved to the old seminary next to the Wawel. They were helped by the continuous stream of refugees—who either came from nearby towns that had been destroyed, or who had just been released from the concentration camps.

In the Jagellonian University, a special organization had just been created: *Bratnia Pomoc*, (Brotherly Aid); and Karol had been elected its vice president. He attempted the impossible, to give a helping hand to everyone. He had received a new sweater, a gift from the Kotlarczyks; and without a moment's hesitation, handed it to a poor man who had come to ask for help.

The atmosphere of freedom was alive, palpable, and infectious. People felt that they were finally out from under that long terrible nightmare—even if they could still see far too many soldiers and tanks all around. There were those individuals who exploited the presence of the Soviets and behaved impudently and arrogantly.

In Lublin, just recently liberated by the Red Army, a Polish Committee of National Liberation had been installed. It was founded in Moscow and staffed by communists of proven loyalty. Boasting official recognition from Stalin, it already claimed the right to carry out the proper functions of a government in place of the one that was still in exile in London.

Few people paid much attention to this turn of events, which had some contradictory features. Nor did anyone make anything of the way some local officials were torpedoed and removed solely because they had no intention of submitting to the new state of affairs. These proved to be the first symptoms of the tragic lot—decided by others—that would befall the Polish nation.

From February 4 through the 12, the Yalta Conference was held on the eastern coast of the Crimea. The war wasn't over yet, but the Great Powers were already agreeing on the split-up of eastern Europe and the Balkans. More precisely, they ratified what the military situation had delineated up to that point. Russia, it must be recalled, had occupied Romania, Bulgaria, Yugoslavia, then Hungary, part of Czechoslovakia, Poland, Prussia, and Silesia.

President Roosevelt was now gravely ill and would die in a few months. At Yalta he did nothing but say yes to Stalin. He was inclined to give in on everything, provided he could get Stalin's consent to create the United Nations, and a commitment to intervene against Japan. Churchill, who had made a series of imprudent concessions to the Russian dictator the year before, found himself with very little room to maneuver. Nevertheless, he tried to reopen the Polish question, which had first prompted the entry of Great Britain and France into the war. "It was for Poland," he emphatically declared, "that we unsheathed the sword."

However, Stalin wouldn't hear of it. He insisted—as if this could be a serious argument—that the conquest of Poland had been very costly to the Soviet army. Then, as if to close the discussion, he declared that, for Russia, the Polish territories represented the surest defense in case a new Hitler ever arose.

He not only won, he triumphed, right down the line. He had an easy time imposing upon the Allies, his geopolitical vision, his proposal for structuring the United Nations, and even his own diktats. For him, every patch of ground that had been "liberated by the Red Flag" would, he said, be "even redder."

The upshot was that the Balkans, and the parts of Europe drained by the Danube—half of Germany, Poland, and the Baltic countries—would be absorbed into the Soviet empire. This came with the formal assurance, however, that "free" elections would be called as soon as possible with a view to creating new "democratic" states. But just as the agreement was being launched, it was already a false promise. Even while the Conference was ending, in Bulgaria three former deputies, nineteen ministers, and eight ex-advisors of King Boris were shot, along with some sixty members of Parliament.

Thus Poland, which had been the first victim of the war, which paid the highest price in numbers of deaths and destruction, which had fought alongside the Allies, and had given enormous support to the struggle for freedom was incredibly discriminated against, penalized, and without ever being consulted, forcibly thrust into the sphere of Soviet influence.

The various delegations had not yet left Yalta when the firebombing of Dresden began. It was Churchill's intention (or someone standing in for him) that there should be a show of force toward Moscow. Instead, it turned out to be an act of pure cruelty, and useless to boot, since Nazism was by now on the verge of collapse. On the evening of February 13—it was Mardi Gras, and the children had just come home with their carnival masks—fourteen hundred planes dropped their bombs on the "Florence of Germany." The city disappeared. To this day, there is still no agreement over the total number of people who died.

The war was at its last gasp. On April 26, American troops arrived in Nuremberg. On the April 21, Zhukov's Russian armies, having occupied Vienna, reached the outskirts of Berlin. Finally, on the afternoon of April 25, at 4:40 P.M. at Torgau on the Elbe, some patrols from the Sixty-Ninth American Infantry Division ran into the advance patrols of the Fifth-Eighth Division of the Red Guard.

Five days later, in his underground bunker dugout in Berlin, sixty feet beneath the Chancellery, Hitler, along with his new bride Eva Braun, committed suicide.

The Third Reich survived the death of its founder by only one week.

The unconditional surrender of Germany was signed at 2:41 in the morning on May 7, 1945. At midnight on May 8—after five years, eight months, and seven days of war—the guns stopped firing. An almost unnatural silence descended upon the battlefields.

Seventy days went by, and the Potsdam Conference opened. That particular little town on the periphery of the capital was chosen because there was hardly a single building still standing in Berlin. It was here that Churchill and Stalin first met with Harry Truman, the new president of the United States.

This time, the war was truly over; and Nazism had been defeated. So the Conference was the symbol of the great victory of freedom. Unfortunately, it will also remain the symbol of the denial of freedom for dozens of nations, and for millions of men and women—this because Potsdam did nothing but sanction and worsen the decisions made at Yalta. Germany was divided in half, in accordance with the Soviet rather than the British plan. The end result was not just the division of Europe, but the creation of an irremediable split between the victors themselves.

What of Poland? The loss of its eastern territories was officially sanctioned up to the Oder-Neisse line. In this way it was "shifted" geographically toward the west; and it lost almost half the territory that had made up its borders between the two world wars; and instead of seeing its legitimate rights as an independent and sovereign nation recognized, it was degraded to the status of a Soviet satellite. In a word, after having bravely and heroically contributed to the final victory, Poland found itself on the side of the vanquished.

Chapter Fourteen

THE HELL OF AUSCHWITZ

They were four Ukrainian soldiers, all very young, still just boys. They all wore white camouflage uniforms and carried machine guns. They emerged warily from the forest, moving out across an endless frozen expanse. They were a reconnaissance patrol from the Sixtieth Soviet Army, simply checking that there weren't anymore Germans left and that the path was clear for the army to advance.

It was January 27, 1945, 3 P.M. on a gray Saturday afternoon that had just been swept with a snowstorm, the four soldiers looked around, perplexed, wondering what that place was. Then, as they moved forward, they gradually began to see and understand.

For the first time, their eyes saw the abyss of horror. In those twenty-five square miles of Auschwitz and Birkenau was the site of the most horrendous crime in history. Their leaders quite probably knew about the Nazi death camps. Churchill and Roosevelt must have known about them since 1943, if not before that time. Representatives of the American Jewish communities had supplied them with extremely precise information. Allied aircraft had taken many well-defined photographs of the camps—but the pictures were labeled top-secret and remained locked up in the desks of high-ranking commanders. The decision had been made not to intervene—as they would try to explain for a long time afterwards—for fear of German reprisals against the prisoners of war.

Was that really true? Anglo-American air power had long controlled the skies of Europe. It need only have bombed the tracks on which the "death trains" ran; that would almost surely have saved hundreds of thousands of human lives.

On that day, January 27, 1945, the four young Ukrainians knew nothing about all of this. They couldn't have known. It was only then that they discovered that hell on earth.

Behind the barbed wire, prisoners were watching the soldiers as if they were specters, were not men, but zombies, with skeletal bodies, expressionless faces, eyes that looked like black holes. These were only some of the 7,650 survivors. The others lay in the wooden huts, unable to move, often with frozen limbs, or sick with tuberculosis.

What most tore at their heart were the children, the boys and girls, all of them reduced to skin and bones. Many weighed less than forty pounds. There were a few hundred of them left of the more than two hundred twenty thousand who had been deported to Auschwitz; they had been left alone, without any family.

The soldiers had to make an enormous effort to continue their painful reconnaissance. They had witnessed many scenes of atrocity in the war, but none were like this. It would have been difficult to describe this scene in any comprehensible way. How, one agonized witness would ask many years later, do you go about "speaking about the unspeakable"?

Here were the ruins of the crematory ovens, all blown up; the last one was detonated only the day before. There were corpses everywhere, more than one hundred thousand of them, whom the Nazi butchers hadn't had time to incinerate. Who knew how many other prisoners had perished of those whom the Nazis dragged on their death march?

In the warehouses, there were thousands of suitcases tagged

with the names and addresses of their owners, three hundred thousand pairs of shoes, a mountain of eyeglasses, of prosthetic limbs, of toys, and a million suits. And then, packaged and ready to be sent back to Germany and rewoven into special fabrics, there was a full seven tons of women's hair!

Anyone who has been to Auschwitz can see all of this displayed behind enormous glass cases, where there lies, although only in the tiniest of amounts, a gloomy visual projection of the number of victims, and hence, of what was the genocide of six million Jews.

At Auschwitz, as well as in the other Polish camps, and in Dachau, Buchenwald, and Mauthausen, a monstrous machine of death had been set in motion. It had been too well organized, too efficient for anyone to believe that the only people behind it were the SS, the jailers, the other immediate perpetrators, and not, regardless of whether out of connivance or constraint, the entire apparatus of the state, from the industries to the railway administration, to the large pharmaceutical houses.

Above and beyond this, it is hard to believe that the driving force behind the death camps was only the insane racism of Hitler, only Germany, and not the entire European context, which had been degraded to the point of allowing such a horrific mass murder to occur.

It's hard to believe that certain Christian communities didn't bear some responsibility: they had showed themselves too fearful, if not indifferent to, or positively supportive of, the persecution that was unleashed long before so systematically and totally against the Jews.

For Poland, it came as a collective shock. Poland had been attacked and occupied by the Nazi army, and more than all the other countries dragged into the war, it had endured the consequences of that war. How are we to not recognize that its destiny, terrible as it was, could not also be equated to a holocaust of a different sort? Even more than that, how are we to not feel profoundly anguished upon realizing that this barbarism had been carried out, above all, right on Polish territory?

Karol was distraught. He had experienced the tragedy only indirectly. Yet, it was so painful and intense an experience for him that, from that moment on, he would forever bear it within himself. It was as if he felt that he, a Pole, the son of a nation that had known the evil of Nazism, had somehow participated in the martyrdom of the Jewish people.

Other groups of human beings had disappeared in the camps: the Gypsies and some Slavic ethnic groups. Protestant ministers, Catholics priests and bishops, Polish and even German ones, had vanished as well, in the wake of the harsh repression to which Hitler had subjected all the churches. By the end of the war, a third of the Polish clergy had either been executed or had died in the concentration camps.

There's a very long list of names, a few of whom are known and many others unknown. All have been united by the experience of having met their death because they were Christians. It was a tragic and, at the same time, exultant experience if one looks at it from the perspective of a life imbued with the radical teachings of the Gospel.

It's sufficient to bring to mind Father Maximilian Kolbe, murdered in Auschwitz, in Block Eleven, after taking the place of another man who was condemned to death. Or the Salesian priest, Jozef Kowalski, from Wojtyla's parish church of Debniki, who was beaten and then drowned because he refused to trample on his own rosary. Or the prior of the convent of Discalced Carmelites in Czerna; Alphonsus Mazurek, who died from a beating he received. It is enough to mention that Dachau became the largest monastery in the world because of the number of religious deportees it housed.

Yet, from the discovery made by the four Ukrainian soldiers on January 27, 1945, it was inevitable to link the memory of Nazi camps to the Shoah, the planned massacre of the children of Israel *simply* because they were Jews; just as it was inevitable to see, in Auschwitz, the "place" that symbolized the absolute limit of scorn for humanity, the absolute negation of the dignity of the human person.

It was also that way for Karol, who lost many Jewish friends and acquaintances, such as the women of the Kluger family, and his two high-school classmates, Zweig and Selinger, who drowned in a river in Siberia where they had been deported.

Karol wouldn't learn that tragic news until after the end of the war—the war in Europe. There was also a war going on in the Pacific, where, for the first and only time, atomic bombs were used in a conflict. Many people today argue that there had been no need for this dire action. With no more ships or war industries, the empire of the Rising Sun was now beaten and ready to surrender. "When will Japan's agony end?" asked the authoritative and objective voice of *The New York Times*.

Nevertheless, those ferocious, homicidal weapons were used. Even back then, an attempt was made to justify this decision. It was said that the United States had recourse to the atomic bomb to put a stop to the war, to save hundreds of thousands of human lives. Their use, however, may have been dictated by other reasons and other exigencies, such as forcing the Soviet Union to accept the superiority of the United States of America and its role as the guarantor of the international order.

The fact remains that on August 6, 1945 (in Europe it was still August 5), a four-engine B-29 (nicknamed *Enola Gay* by its commander in honor of his mother), took off with the atomic bomb aboard. In an even worse bit of bad taste, it was called "Little Boy." Its initial target was selected by chance or, more precisely, by the prevailing weather conditions, which decreed the death sentence upon Hiroshima, where it was "mostly clear, with ten miles visibility."

First Hiroshima, and then Nagasaki, were reduced to nothing by a fiery wind, a "thunderous flash," "a big blue flash," as seen by the "lucky ones" who lived to tell about it. Never had it happened before that, in barely three days, so many people died together at the very same instant. Many of those who survived were condemned to an existence marked forever by the after-effects of atomic radiation.

Between the time of the two explosions, Moscow took the opportunity to declare war on Japan; its troops invaded Manchuria and continued to advance even after the surrender was announced by Emperor Hirohito. Finally, the guns fell silent everywhere; and only then did the vastness of horror in this twentieth-century apocalypse begin to be revealed.

The war had caused fifty-five million deaths. Beyond that figure, there were the missing and those who died of either hunger or due to the cold; their exact number could never be known. The Soviet Union alone had thirty-seven million victims, Germany had around four million; Poland lost more than a million soldiers and five million civilians, more than half of them Jews.

That wasn't all. On that disastrous balance sheet, one also had to include entire populations who had been subjected to forced removal from one part of Europe to another, who at a single stroke found themselves without a home, country, or roots. No less depressing was the story of mass destruction: thousands of cities were leveled; many towns were so far gone that they could no longer be rebuilt; and the very equilibrium of nature had suffered such severe alterations that they were often beyond repair.

The war was over; and a black, impenetrable blanket had descended on the destiny of countless people. Something of this would become known many years later, as happened to Karol with his loss of friends and schoolmates.

Galuszka, the youngest in their class in Wadowice, had joined the Uhlans, the regiment of the Polish cavalry, and had been killed at the age of eighteen shortly after the war began, near the western front. Gajczak also died during the first days of the German invasion, shot down with his plane. The great Czuprynski, the famous Don Juan of the *gymnasium*, had stepped on a mine in Ancona, shortly after taking part in the victorious battle of Montecassino.

So many others, however, had just disappeared, swallowed up in nothingness. They fell on various fronts, with the Polish National Army, or at Tobruk, or they died in the Nazi death camps, or in the Soviet gulags in Siberia.

At that same time, Karol, as if obliged by circumstances, began to wonder why he had been spared from all that had happened. Why had so many of his friends lost their lives when he hadn't?

Among the answers that he tried to supply, he initially thought that the reason he had been saved could be attributed to fate, or fortune, or simply to chance. He told himself it was also true that "there is nothing accidental in God's plans." In any event, the great evil of war, with all its burden of tragedy and suffering, marked Karol's existence forever. His choice had been made.

Twenty-seven years after they had last seen each other, Karol unexpectedly met one of his dearest Jewish friends, Jerzy Kluger in Rome. Kluger had never returned to Poland, especially after he learned about the tragic end his family members had met in Auschwitz. He was married and had two daughters. After working in England, he had moved to Italy. Karol and Jerzy each thought the other was dead; but instead they had miraculously found each other again.

Chapter Fifteen

THE FIRST MASS

Karol had naturally chosen the cathedral of Cracow, on the Wawel. His first Mass could be celebrated only in the sanctuary where the history of Poland had been written—the history of its religious tradition, and of its martyr-dom, its national and civilian history, the history of its culture, its heroism, and of the centuries-long, unending struggle to win back its lost and oppressed heritage.

His new life could only begin from there, from the Wawel, to express the particular bond that had matured with all the memories of the nation, and to render homage to all those who had exerted an important influence on its Christian and patri-otic formation—the "great spirits," as he called them. That meant the spiritual guides, such as Bishop Stanislas, all the kings and queens who had been crowned and buried there, like Wladyslaw Lokietek or Blessed Hedwig; and the great poets, like Mickiewicz and Slowacki, the great leaders like Kosciuszko and Poniatowski.

Never did Karol feel that he had to pray for his poor home-land, betrayed once more, scorned and treated as the last coun-try on earth, as much as he did in that special moment when he became a new priest. He felt, who knows why, that his priestly mission, in a future that loomed ever more darkly, would be

108

tightly tied to the fortunes of Poland and, in a special way, with the defense and promotion of the dignity of the human person.

On the previous day—November 1, 1946—he had been ordained a priest or, as Saint Paul says, a minister of the "mysteries of God." In the middle of the chapel of the archbishop's palace, he, Karol, was the only one to be ordained. Prostrate on the ground, his face on the floor, his arms opened in the form of a cross, as a sign of total submission to God and of full responsibility to undertake the ministry that would soon be entrusted to him. As the litany of the saints was intoned, he managed to collect himself and think about the profound meaning of what was happening: an event that represented the definitive seal on the path he had traversed in those last years.

He knelt down before Archbishop Sapieha; and the archbishop, standing in silence, laid his hands on his head. At that point, as he listened to the ancient hymn of the Church, *Veni Creator Spiritus*, Karol had a strange sensation: as if an "effusion of grace" was actually pouring down from on high, as if the Creator Spirit had in fact come down, there, to the center of the chapel. Then, at that precise instant, he finally understood that his life had changed, forever.

In February, Archbishop Sapieha had gone to Rome to receive the cardinal's hat from Pius XII. Upon his return, when he stepped off the train and got into his car, dozens of students hoisted the vehicle on their shoulders and carried it to the old city, to the church of Saint Mary, in Market Square. It was meant to be an acknowledgment by Poland, after the one conferred by the pope, of the archbishop's pastoral courage and powerful testimony in the face of Nazism. It was certainly no accident that, in the congratulatory speech he later delivered at the seminary, Karol would refer to the homily by a nineteenth-century hero on the religious significance of patriotism.

Once the celebration was over, Cardinal Sapieha went immediately to work. The serious rifts that the war had caused in the Catholic community had to be healed; vital new energy had to be pumped into its structures and pastoral methods. Before all else, a remedy had to be found for the scarcity of clergy. "The Church," the archbishop had said, "is facing difficult times; and hence it must be able to count on well-prepared priests— priests who know how to proclaim Christ to the people, but also to be close to their problems, whether they are personal, family related, or social."

For this reason, Sapieha had decided to speed up Wojtyla's ordination, so he could send him immediately to Rome to study for a doctorate in theology. Without giving it much thought, he had chosen a rather unusual date for a ceremony of this kind: the feast of All Saints. Thus, on that morning, he had placed his hands on the young deacon's head, consecrating him a priest forever.

Twenty-four hours later there came Karol's first Mass in the Wawel cathedral. Actually, he celebrated three Masses, as the custom allowed on All Souls' Day; and Karol said all three in the Romanesque crypt of Saint Leonard, which was so charged with history and located near the royal tombs. Almost side-by-side with the altar lay the mortal remains of two of Poland's most famous kings: Michael Korybut Wisnowiecki and John III Sobieski, who in 1683 had halted the Turkish advance beneath the walls of Vienna, thereby saving all of Europe.

Now, in the coming weeks and months, another kind of "siege" was expected, perhaps even more menacing than the one the Ottoman troops had launched against the Austrian capital. Poland, in fact, was living in an atmosphere of grave uncertainty. The new social and political system, although it had a veneer of democracy, was already showing the first signs of a steady devolution into a totalitarian regime and, even more than that, into one that was completely submissive to the Kremlin and its directives.

The Lublin Committee of National Liberation had become a real, though provisional, government, headed by Boleslaw Bierut, a hardline Soviet communist. After long negotiations with Moscow, the British and Americans managed to get the vice presidency for Mikolajczyk, who had represented Poland in exile. It was too ambiguous and too precarious a solution to justify either the hope that it could last or, even somewhat less than that, the illusion that it would be respected by the Soviets.

That was why, in this situation swarming with new dangers, the Wawel cathedral, now finally reopened to the public, seemed to be an oasis—the only oasis—of authentic freedom. For this reason as well, Karol wanted to pray intensely for his homeland, for the Polish people.

As he began his first Mass, he was visibly agitated, moved, and completely absorbed by what would have to be done. From that day onward, the celebration of the Eucharist would become the center of his life, the most important and sacred moment of every day.

Fortunately, he had Don Figlewicz, his confessor, by his side to guide him through the words and gestures. He was the *manuductor*, as the master of liturgical ceremonies used to be called. But toward the end, seeing that the new priest was doing fine, he told him, "Now go on by yourself."

Serving the Mass as his "altar boy" was the seminarian Malinksi, whom he had known since the days of the Living Rosary; but there was only a small group of family and friends in the congregation: Maria Wiadrowska, the elder sister of Karol's mother and his godmother; the Kotlarczyks, the Kydrynskis, Mrs. Szkocki, as well as Halina the actress; and Tadeusz Kwiatkowski, who had married and already had a beautiful little girl, Monika Katarzyna.

The only one missing, of all people, was Jan Tyranowski, the one person who had played a large part in Wojtyla's decision to become a priest. The tailor-catechist had been hospitalized with a nasty disease caused by the poorly healed infection in his arm, which eventually had to be amputated. A few months later Jan would die; he was only forty-seven years old. Right to the very end, despite his atrocious suffering, he maintained an extraordinary serenity.

For priestly ordinations it was the custom to print up special engraved announcements to be distributed to relatives and friends in remembrance of the day. For financial reasons, it was not possible to do this, so Karol gave out holy cards. On each card he had written a verse taken from the Gospel of Luke: "*Fecit mihi magna*": "He has done great things for me." Everyone appreciated the little souvenir.

After the first Masses, there were many others: in the Salesian church in the Debniki district where Karol had lived with his father, in the parish church of Wadowice where he had been baptized, and once more up in the Wawel cathedral, at the altar of Saint Stanislas. On that occasion, his friends from the Rhapsodic Theater had come along with his old workmates from the quarry and the Solvay factory, who presented him with a cassock, as well as the surviving members of the underground movement *Unia*, who were already having serious troubles with the constant pressure from the communist authorities.

Evidently, those who had fought for the survival of Poland during the Nazi occupation, for its return to freedom and independence, no longer had any civil rights in a country headed for a new dictatorship.

The day of departure was now drawing near. Karol barely had time to administer the sacrament of baptism—the first in his life—to Halina's and Tadeusz's daughter in the church of Saint Anne. He also found a way to attend a performance of his old theater company. Finally, on November 15, in a state of high excitement, together with a younger colleague named Starowieyski, he boarded the train for Paris.

It was the first time he had crossed the Polish border. Seated by the window he didn't want to miss anything. Even if only on the fly, he began to get acquainted with countries he had just read about in geography books. The stops were short, too short; but even so, you could imagine that you were seeing the world.

Prague was splendid and intriguing. Karol had heard people talk especially about the old city, with the two greatest symbols of Church and state up on the hill next to each other: the cathedral of Saint Vitus and the ancient residence of the kings of Bohemia.

The train then passed through Nuremberg, a name that recalled the most terrible acts of the Second World War. A few weeks before, the war crimes trial in that city had ended, and the Nazi leaders had been executed.

On the night of October 16, Hans Frank, the ruthless governor general of Poland, had gone up on the scaffold, too. Before dying, he admitted to some of his crimes, saying that he had a "demon" within him. He had repented, and had even asked for forgiveness from God, whom he claimed to have rediscovered in the end.

The journey continued. Strasbourg and then Paris, marvelous Paris, but only for a very short layover, with just enough time to spend the night in the Polish seminary. The next day, at the crack of dawn, he had to rush to the station to catch another train, this time headed directly to Rome.

Karol looked at the landscapes slipping past him and thought about the time when he would return to his country. Who knew what he would find then?

Under Nazism, everything had come to a halt, even pastoral work. And now thicker and thicker storm clouds seemed to be gathering over the future of the Church. Terrifying reports were drifting in from the Soviet Union about the persecution of believers and Christian communities. In nearby Lithuania, a bishop named Borisevicius had been condemned to death and shot. Another, Ramanauskas, had been deported to Siberia. Still, Karol did not despair.

He thought back to the conversation he once had with a young Russian soldier, whom he had met by chance in Cracow, the morning after the liberation. Karol knew Russian fairly well, and so they had been able to talk for hours.

"The Russian soldier," Wojtyla would relate many years afterwards, "did not become a seminarian; but in the course of the discussion, I learned a great deal about the way God makes inroads into the thoughts of people who live under conditions of systematic denial of his existence. My interlocutor had never set foot in an orthodox church as an adult, but vaguely remembered having gone with his mother to one as a baby. In contrast, both in school and at work he had constantly heard the existence of God denied."

The soldier insisted several times on one point. "In our country," he said, "they keep repeating that God doesn't exist. But I've always known that he does exist, and I'd like to learn more about him."

Back then, Karol had become convinced that the "truth about God" is written in the spirit of simple people who are neither philosophers nor scientists; and no ideology could extinguish that truth in the human heart.

At that very moment, Karol glimpsed in the distance the dim outlines of a city. It was Rome, coming to meet him.

Chapter Sixteen

DISCOVERING ROME

B efore Karol left Cracow, the rector of the seminary had repeated to him *ad nauseam*: "Yes, sure, you'll have to study, but you have to get to know Rome too." And Karol followed his advice to the letter.

He began, of course, with the Vatican, where he went one Sunday for a beatification ceremony. It was the first time that he had seen Saint Peter's up close, and the first time he entered. He suddenly felt a strong, intense, deeply emotional impression, although it was mixed in with some confusion over the way the rite was performed in those days. A cardinal was presiding, and only in the afternoon did the pope—Pope Pius XII—come down to Saint Peter's to recite a prayer to the newly beatified person.

And then, day after day, Karol continued his exploring. He set out to discover Rome in its most diverse aspects: the Rome of the catacombs, the martyrs, and the thousand churches; the Rome of the great works of art and monuments; but also the more touristic Rome, the Rome of Trastevere, the Piazza Navona, and the Trevi Fountain.

At the same time, taking an approach that was perhaps slower, but continuous and progressive, he succeeded in "learning" Rome, that is, loving it, understanding its deepest spirit, until he made his way into that dimension of universality that would remain attached to him like a second skin, and that would bring him to look upon the Church, the world, and history against a boundless horizon, with no barriers or limits of any kind, and, above all, without blinders.

Karol was housed in the Belgian College, on the via del Quirinale, and took his theology courses at the Angelicum, the university run by the Dominicans at the beginning of the via Nazionale. He stopped to pray at Sant'Andrea, which enshrines the relics of a Polish saint, Stanislas Kostka, to whom Karol's parish church in the Debniki district of Cracow was consecrated. In that Jesuit church he often found German seminarians with their gaudy red soutanes. He was struck by the fact that in the heart of Christendom, the various nationalities, once dressed in the uniforms of war, quickly found themselves united together.

Thus, every day held a new surprise, a fresh discovery. One has to realize that immediately after the war, Rome was a city overflowing with violence and poverty, with few stores open and the black market in charge. Only a few cars were driven around with tires that were mostly recycled from American jeeps, and parts patched on with screws and bolts.

It was a Rome that—like the rest of Italy—was swept back and forth by the disputes arising after the referendum on the monarchy and the republic, with the "whodunit" atmosphere that prevailed during the long uncertainty before the final results were made public. Karol had nothing to say about this. For him these were the normal sparks from a political debate in a free democratic government—the total opposite of what was happening in his own country.

In Poland, the communists had already manipulated the referendum of 1946, employing the same methods they would use in the elections of January 1947.

On the eve of the voting, they unleashed their police cadres to deal with the secret ballot, even using ex-members of the national army. The latter were accused of collaboration simply because they hadn't fought alongside the Soviets against the Nazis. Then the repression shifted to the countryside. The communists targeted the main opposition, the peasant party, led by Stanislaw Mikolajczyk; and almost sixty thousand of its militants were arrested.

Once the socialists were forcibly absorbed, a single party was created, the POUP, United Polish Workers Party, thereby banishing even the last semblance of pluralism. Political opponents were driven out of the country. And to fill the post of Minister of Defense and commander in chief of the army, a marshal was sent from Moscow, Konstanty Rokossowski, the same man who had halted the Red Army at the Vistula River and hadn't fired a shot as he stood back and let the Germans destroy Warsaw.

Poland was truly finished. After the defeat of Nazism, the country had barely begun to taste the sweetness of freedom again, only to plunge suddenly and hopelessly under another dictatorship.

In those days Karol didn't show any special interest in political problems; but he obviously couldn't help being worried by what was going on in Poland, and what he was learning from the newspapers and letters from his friends. Still, he hoped to find out for himself, thinking he would return home for his vacation. But Cardinal Sapieha had decided otherwise. He wrote to Wojtyla and the other Polish student, Starowieyski, to use that time to become familiar with Catholic life in a few other countries of western Europe.

They had already seen half of Italy. They had gone to Assisi, guided by the Danish writer, Joergensen's biography of Saint Francis. From there, they went to Montecassino, in memory of the many Polish soldiers who had fallen there; and to San Giovanni Rotondo, where they went to have their confession heard by Padre Pio, whom they found to be "very simple, clear, and concise." Karol was stunned to see how much the Capuchin priest suffered from his stigmata while celebrating Mass.

At that point they began to turn their attention to Europe. For their first stop, they made the obvious choice of France. In Paris they discovered the Metro, which was always jammed. But most of all they discovered a city that was more cheerful than Rome, where the people wanted to have fun and were in a hurry to forget the tragedy of the war. At the same time, Paris was a city where daring, forward-looking experiments in pastoral care were being made, even if they were looked upon with suspicion by certain ecclesiastical circles in Rome.

The two young Poles made contact with the worker priests, who went off to the factories and tried to reestablish a dialogue between the Church and the world through their testimony. They also got to know the priests of the *Mission de Paris*, which had started a new type of evangelization to recover the suburbs. These were two examples of how the cry of alarm, first sent out by a book entitled *La France, pays de mission?* had not fallen on deaf ears. The authors, Fathers Godin and Daniel, have shown how far the de-Christianization of the French society had gone.

For Karol it was a very important lesson. He realized that the crisis in France was, in reality, the anticipation of a challenge that all of Catholicism would eventually have to face. He also saw that out of that situation a new image of the Church was emerging—a Church no longer frozen by its fears, no longer turned in upon itself, but a Church that was beginning to move out of its sacred enclosures, to go forth to meet—as the archbishop of Paris, Suhard, used to say—the population that no longer "thought like Christians."

After France, they moved on to the Church in Holland, which had a sturdy organization, both internally and in its mission outreach. From there they visited Belgium, where Karol spent a month near Charleroi attending to Polish miners and their families who lived there.

Still in Belgium, he could see directly how the *Jeunesse Ouvrière Chrétienne* operated: while in Rome he talked about the movement with its founder, Father Jözef Cardijn. The JOC was dedicated to the spiritual and professional training of young people and, in particular, of young workers. It had promoted a close relationship, or rather a reciprocal coordination, between priestly service and the apostolate of the laity. This too was an extremely interesting experience for Wojtyla, who had a vision of the priesthood that was anything but clerical.

He returned to Rome with a large suitcase full of discoveries, impressions, and ideas. He had immersed himself in Christian Europe, the world of marvelous Gothic cathedrals and of so many new ecclesiastical realities. But he also had come to know a Europe in ferment, in search of an identity after the devastation of the war, and already attacked in its heart by secularism. For starters, there would be a need for renewed evangelization, with new pastoral formats, open to a greater presence of lay people and, hence, to greater freedom and responsibility for lay people within the Church.

Karol must have had something like this in mind when, while preparing his thesis on "Faith According to Saint John of the Cross," he emphasized the personal nature of the encounter of man with God. That, as he saw it, meant that the person must enjoy freedom, because one can enter an authentic relationship of mutual self-giving only if one is free.

His thesis advisor, Father Réginald Garrigou-Lagrange, didn't quite agree. He was the pre-eminent figure among the professors at the Angelicum; but he, too, even if less so than the others, was bound by an extremely rigorous neo-Scholasticism, which presented itself as an alternative to modern philosophical systems instead of seeking contacts with the new trends. In any case, Wojtyla did brilliantly on his doctoral exams, obtaining the highest possible grade—fifty out of fifty—on the oral examination.

Karol left Rome in June 1947, satisfied with the past two years, which had been so full and profitable. He felt profoundly changed and more mature, thanks to the greater confidence that he now had in his theological training and to the deeper levels he had reached in his own priesthood and in the Church itself, with all its diverse expressions. The experience of the worker priests, which he considered "of enormous interest," was the topic he addressed in the first of a series of articles that he began to publish in the *Tygodnik Powszechny*, the famous and combative Cracow weekly run by Jerzy Turowicz.

But, on the way back, he was surprised by an ugly incident. At the Polish frontier the train stopped, abruptly slamming on the brakes. Two soldiers strode in, first scanning the passports suspiciously, then peppering the passengers with questions. Where were they coming from? Why had they been abroad? And so forth. On the way out there hadn't been that sort of intense scrutiny. Obviously things were changing, and not for the better.

In that very same time period, the communist world was also in turmoil: Tito had been "excommunicated," and Yugoslavia was expelled from the Cominform. To be sure, the institutional structures of this Balkan version of socialism continued to closely follow those of the Soviet Union. Still the mere prospect of any kind of diversity, since it might mean a quest for greater autonomy from Moscow, sent waves of panic among the leaders of world communism.

Meanwhile, attacks against believers and the churches were spreading almost everywhere. For Marxism and its concept of the state, the existence of an extraneous "power," and, even more than that, one linked with an international body such as the Holy See, was, to put it mildly, intolerable. Hence, behind the hardening of the antireligious campaign lay the furious reaction of Moscow as it witnessed the failure of its attempt to create national churches detached from the Vatican, and hence easy to check up on and manipulate.

The archbishop of Zagreb, Alojzije Stepinac, was one of the first to oppose this maneuver and had paid a high price for it. In fact, it was in "breakaway" Yugoslavia, with its so-called liberal communism, that the this ignoble process had been set in motion. Arrested and charged with complicity with the regime of Ante Pavelic, the archbishop had been condemned to sixteen years of hard labor.

In Ukraine, the Greek Catholic Church had been suppressed and incorporated into the Orthodox Church. Its spiritual head, Josyp Slipyj, the Metropolitan of Lviv, had refused to cut his ties with Rome. He, too, had been condemned and was already in the third of his eighteen years of forced detention.

In Poland, the situation was not so dramatic. But many people recalled that Stalin had once joked that introducing communism into that country would be like "training a cow to wear a saddle." That is, it would be very hard to subdue and tame a nation that was predominantly Catholic. But now, with Poland submerged in the Soviet empire and completely defenseless, the new czar would try. Stalin would surely try.

Chapter Seventeen

A COUNTRY PARISH

Karol was still a long way off, but he finally managed to see it. He was walking through the open country, the splendid countryside of Marszowice, among the fields of grain now ripe for the harvest, when a church suddenly loomed into view. It must have been small, but all the same, it dominated the network of farmhouses that once was rather compact, but had spread, and finally was lost in the surrounding plain.

It was the parish church of Niegowic, a little village on the farthest outskirts of Cracow, at the foot of the Carpathians. His first parish! His first pastoral work! And there he would begin to carry out his priestly ministry, no longer just bending over books, no longer just theorizing, but caught up in the real everyday life of a people, of a Christian community.

He had barely come back from Rome when he found the letter from Cardinal Sapieha containing the *aplikata*, or notice of his assignment. The archbishop had sent him as a vicar to a fairly remote church, hidden in the countryside; but it was an excellent "laboratory" for the initiation of young priests. It had a highly experienced pastor, Don Buzala. The parish, dedicated to the Assumption of Our Lady, was like a big family; and its religious values were still deeply rooted in the life of the people.

That day, July 28, 1948, Karol had set out early in the morning, full of curiosity and, above all, intensely excited. Niegowic is fifteen miles from Cracow, located a little way past the salt mines of Wieliczka; but the trip would have lasted an eternity. The bus took quite a while to get to Gdow. And at Gdow the bus line ended, and one had to continue on foot.

At this point in time, Wojtyla was as skinny as a rail; and he was dragging behind him an old suitcase with very little clothing but an enormous number of books—who knew how much the whole thing weighed? A horse-drawn wagon passed; the peasant took pity on him and offered a ride. After three or four kilometers, the peasant told him that he'd reach his destination faster by taking that shortcut on the right. The young priest walked across the luxuriant field, with the harvest swaying beneath the gusts of wind, until he saw the bell tower and the church.

He felt the urge to kneel down and kiss the earth. It was a gesture that he had learned from Saint Jean-Marie Vianney, the Curé d'Ars. The year before, during his visit to France, he had made a point of stopping at Ars, to pray at the tomb of the saint whom he considered one of his priestly models, especially as a confessor. And that kiss of the earth, as a sign of respect and homage to the people and traditions of a given place, would always remain part of his pastoral "baggage."

The pastor gave him a very cordial welcome, and Karol didn't take long to feel at home, even though, to be truthful, one had to admit that Niegowic was in a bad state. There was no electricity, there were no sewers, and a recent flood had ruined both fields and roads. For that reason in the first days, and especially in the winter, with the cold, he had problems carrying out his main occupation, which was teaching religion.

There was one parish church for all fourteen villages within a radius of some six miles; and scattered over that territory were the five elementary schools he had to oversee. He was driven around in a little wagon or a calash. If the weather was good, he also had the possibility of reading a book. But when the temperature went below freezing, and the snow blocked the paths, the trip became an adventure.

When he managed to arrive at his destination, he had another, even more difficult problem: how to control a mob of wild, shouting children. Only once did the teacher succeed in keeping them all still and quiet. "To this day," he would remember many years later, "I sometimes find myself thinking back to the thoughtful silence that reigned in the class during Lent when I spoke about the passion of the Lord."

But Karol did more than teach religion. Every day, of course, he said Mass. He spent long hours in the confessional where, he said, he could have a direct, intimate relationship with souls. He administered baptism, all told, about fifty times. He celebrated some marriages, after personally preparing the engaged couples. He visited the sick, bringing, if necessary, extreme unction. And he accompanied to the little cemetery those who had finished their earthly journey.

As Christmas drew near, he began making the rounds of family visits, even going to see those who lived a long way off. He arrived in his increasingly threadbare overcoat, and his guests gave him the seat of honor in the dining room. He listened to everyone, and they prayed together. Finally, he blessed the house, and even went outside to bless the farm animals. And so it went, for all of the fourteen villages in the parish.

The people greeted him on the street with a warm, "Praised be Jesus Christ." At first they took him for a wet-behind-the-ears professor, someone who had studied and done nothing else, with no pastoral experience. But they quickly got to know him better and then to love him. He was a special priest: he gave everything that he thought might be helpful. One time he got a present of a pillow and a quilt, which he immediately passed on to a poor woman who had been robbed; and he went back to sleeping on a bare bed.

Day after day, Karol learned not just to "act like a priest," but he invented, so to speak, his own pastoral style, which in the years to come, he would refine and develop. He managed to win people's confidence, to talk about their problems, even if they were strictly human and personal, while remaining himself, that is, a priest. And that was without ever selling short his own identity, without ever succumbing to the risk of reducing his ministry to an official routine, and becoming a simple "employee" of the sacred.

And then, he had his own striking way of celebrating Mass. He never rushed through any of the gestures, but, to the contrary, tried to fully express their significance and symbolism. He spoke every word with emphasis, consciously, so that the announcement it contained could be grasped by everyone. The pauses were always long and thoughtful: the faithful present had to feel that they were really participating in what is considered the greatest mystery of the Christian faith.

Cracow was nearby; fifteen miles was nothing. Nevertheless, in Niegowic, one could still lead a serene, tranquil life separated from the trauma of a city and country where the contradictions of the convulsive transformation of Polish society were simply exploding. Hundreds of thousands of people had returned from the work camps of the Third Reich. Another million and a half had been moved from the eastern territories, which were now part of the USSR, to the western one, which had been recovered by the expulsion of a large part of their German population.

Meanwhile, in Poland, as in the rest of the other satellite countries of the empire, the construction of the new socialist state had commenced. And the model was borrowed in every detail from the Soviets: a single party, economic centralization, intensive development of industry, especially of heavy industry, and gradual elimination of any kind of private property, as well as of entrepreneurial and handicraft activities.

The process of "Sovietization" marched step for step with the repression. First, there was a ruthless elimination of the upper echelons of the prewar army. Then, the internal adversaries were attacked, that is the nationalist wing of the United Polish Workers Party. Wladislaw Gomulka, who was also vice president of the Council, was accused of "rightist deviation," and expelled from the POUP, imprisoned and, along with him, hundreds of party leaders and thousands of militants. It was somewhat reminiscent of what happened in the Soviet Union in the days of Trotskyism.

But the shift of society toward Marxism reached its most virulent stage in the area of ideology and culture. Here, inevitably, the clash with the Church was especially bitter. The Church had remained alone in the trenches, fighting to preserve the national and Christian patrimony and to defend the rights and freedoms of the people.

But it wasn't that way everywhere. In other countries, where the Catholic community was weaker, or at least not so well organized and less firmly integrated into the life of the larger society, persecution was more violent and direct, particularly against the clergy. Between imprisonments, deportations, and killings, some bishoprics were literally wiped out. This had already happened under the Nazis; but now, perhaps, it was even worse.

In Albania, the primate of the Church, Monsignor Taci, the archbishop of Scutari, died while in the hands of the secret police. Similarly, the archbishop of Durazzo, Prendushi, who had been condemned to thirty years at hard labor, died, probably as the result of torture. Two other bishops were shot. And Albania set out to become the first officially atheistic state in the world.

In Lithuania, the bishops were arrested or killed; 50 percent of the clergy were deported to the gulags. In Romania, the Greek Catholic Church was the first to be banned, then the Latin rite Church was liquidated; and the representatives of the Orthodox community didn't say a single word in their defense, not a word of solidarity for their Christian brothers.

In Hungary, after the clash over the nationalization of the

religious schools, the situation got out of control on the feast of Saint Stephen. The primate, Cardinal Joszef Mindszenty, was arrested by the political police, accused of plotting against the republic and of complicity with American imperialism. Then he was drugged, forced to confess to nonexistent crimes, and finally condemned to life imprisonment.

In Poland, by contrast, the regime had recourse to different methods. First, it tried, in vain, to create a Church separate from Rome. Then, it sought to divide the Church by giving special treatment to "patriotic priests" and to the pro-communist association *Pax*, which was officially recognized. But, above all, the regime worked to undermine the foundations of the Church through bureaucratic harassment, such as the confiscation of land, rationing paper for publications, imposing military service on seminarians, and closing church associations, especially youth groups. And that was just what they tried to do even in small villages like Niegowic.

Karol had managed to get on friendly terms with the children and young people of the parish. He had started a theater group, and given a performance. He organized soccer and volleyball tournaments. He took the whole group to Cracow and on hikes. When the sun went down, they lit campfires, sang songs, prayed, and discussed all sorts of things, not just religion.

All of this obviously was bound to displease the communist authorities. And at a certain point a number of suspicious-looking characters who no one had ever seen before showed up in the village; they were spies. But instead of launching a frontal attack on Wojtyla, they tried to create a vacuum around him by drawing the young people away from him, and then setting up a different, politically oriented organization. They used the usual technique: before turning to violence, make use of the "instruments" for corrupting and infiltrating the enemy.

They began with Stanislaw Wyporek, one of the young people who went most often to see the vicar—among other things

he was giving Wojtyla secretarial help. Every morning he came
to the rectory to type (by the hunt-and-peck method) his thesis
on Saint John of the Cross. The agents approached young
Wyporek to get information about the group, which they could
then use to blackmail the individual members. But Stanislaw
refused to collaborate; and so one night they forced him into a
car, took him to a nearby village, and thrashed him.

Stanislaw reappeared in Niegowic the next morning. He
hadn't given anyone away, but he was covered with bruises and
in a state of shock. Karol went to console him and thanked him
for his loyalty and courage. "If they show up again," he said,
"just tell the truth. Tell them what the boys in the parish do.
There's nothing to hide. And then, don't worry, they'll do themselves in."

Later, he talked with the other youngsters about what had
happened. He repeated the same advice, but for the first time,
to practically everyone's surprise, he added a somewhat political judgment. "Socialism," he explained, "isn't against the teachings of the Church, but the methods of the communists are
against the Church. Communism imposes the materialistic idea
of the people, and tortures the nation."

Some years later Wyporek visited the former vicar, and was
astonished to see, in his library, many works by Marx and Lenin.
"What!" he asked jokingly, "Did you convert to a different ideology?" To which Karol replied: "My dear Stanislaw, if you
want to understand the enemy, you have to know what he has
written!"

Chapter Eighteen

Young People
Against the Lie

At the beginning of the 1950s, a book was published entitled *The Captive Mind*. It was authored by the Polish writer Czeslaw Milosz, the future Nobel prize winner for literature. At first, the book was practically banned; only much later did it win wide appreciation and become famous. In it, Milosz has a high-ranking communist party functionary say: "When the masses begin to understand that no one is responsible, they fall into apathy; and molding them isn't difficult anymore."

Those words mirrored what was going on at that time in Poland. It was the period of Stalinist terror, of the purges and secret accusations. Above all, it was a time when the lie ruled with absolute sovereignty. With the lie, an immense and growing stream of hypocrisy flowed into the nation.

The history of Poland was completely rewritten and manipulated by the regime. For example, General Anders, the hero of Montecassino, was stripped of his citizenship, and his name disappeared from books. But there were worse happenings yet to come. From many witnesses it now seems confirmed that the organized massacre, the pogrom of Kielce, which cost the lives

of fifty Jews, was originally instigated by the communists themselves. At that point, it served their interests to dump the accu-
sation of anti-Semitism on their political opponents in order to
discredit them internationally. In Poland, there was an obses-
sive, hammering ideology that falsified everything and twisted
reality, with the result that people's consciences were collectively
put to sleep. As Milosz said, their minds were "captive," minds
that had been seduced by sociopolitical messianic visions and
accepted totalitarian terror in exchange for a hypothetical future. Thus, society wound up confusing the very meaning of
liberty, human rights, and its own collective responsibility.

If so many people who were obliged to live in constant fear
had lowered their guard, conformed, and no longer hoped for
anything, the least of which was for help from the West, there
were, nevertheless, many young people who, although they did
not yet come out into the open, were reacting against this state
of things. Still more basically, they weren't prepared to adopt
for themselves any crudely materialistic conception of life and
history such as that in Marxism.

So Wojtyla found fertile terrain when he approached the
world of young people. After spending only eight months in
Niegowic, in the country on the outskirts of Cracow, he had
been transferred to Saint Florian, a centrally located parish near
the old city. It was one of the most active and vital parishes,
frequented by members of the Catholic intelligentsia. There, as
in the church of Saint Anne, a pastoral center was opened up
for university students.

At first, it was a little difficult to enter that new environ-
ment, which was still uncharted territory. Karol taught religion
in a lyceum and spent many hours in the confessional. Finally,
one day the Sisters of the Holy Family, who ran a girls' prep
school, decided to invite him to hold a series of discussions with
their students. That's how it began, almost by chance. But then
the adolescent grapevine did the rest, and very quickly.

The girls were joined by male students. Then still others

came; and they were all instantly won over, fascinated by the new chaplain. It was the first time that a priest, instead of talking only about God, religion, and the Church, also addressed various aspects of their lives as young people. And he didn't dodge the touchiest issues, such as how to face and solve problems in love and marriage, problems with work and relationships with adults.

He wasn't like the other priests, who repeated the usual, predictable things, always giving them a thick clerical flavoring. Nor was he like the professors in the university, who were afraid to speak out because of the spies circulating in the halls.

Wojtyla had his own personal method: he challenged atheism, starting from the reality of the young people's lives. He didn't attack Marxism directly; but by the mere fact that he showed the stunning contradictions between it and their needs and lives, he essentially demolished Marxist ideology from within.

His audiences continued to grow; soon the Thursday conferences were no longer enough. The young people were thirsty for different words, for true and believable words; they needed guides and wanted to feel their near and friendly presence. It was then that Karol thought back to what he had seen, years before, on his trips through Europe, and to the need he had noticed for new educational and pastoral methods. That was his starting point for inventing the so-called apostolate of the excursion.

He began by taking boys and girls together on hikes into the mountains, for camping and skiing trips, and for canoeing on the lakes in summertime. Occasionally these trips lasted for a couple of weeks. The participants would gather around a fire or after an outdoor Mass; afterwards, they would continue to reflect about God, spirituality, or the human soul, but also about the concrete problems that they encountered in their daily lives.

For those days, this was a pioneering experience. In fact, at first they were viewed with a certain distrust by the parents themselves. The police took a still dimmer view of the practice, since they saw conspiracies everywhere and imagined the threat of revolt in every little gathering. To avoid attracting attention, Wojtyla dressed in mufti (civilian clothes) while on the outings. His students called him *Wujek* (uncle). They were *Paczka*, the gang.

In the Gospel, the young people continued to find a meaningful reference point for their existence. For his part, Karol discovered the importance of youth as the crucial period for the personalization of human life and, hence, for the construction of a serious existential project. At the same time, he realized that the desire for self-affirmation particular to the young people mustn't be understood as legitimizing everything without exception. Rather, he was convinced that the young people themselves would be the first to reject this, "They're also ready to be corrected; they want to be told yes or no."

Following up on this, Wojtyla launched a program of marriage preparation, the first of its kind in the diocese of Cracow. He organized courses for those who were engaged and celebrated many marriages, at least one per week for several years. He regularly kept in touch with the newly married couples, especially after the births of their children. He himself would baptize them and, for as long as he could, he often went to see them and talked to their parents.

So a new gathering took shape, the *Rodzinka,* or "little family." The *Rodzinka* was progressively fused with the first pastoral front, that of the young people, to the point that it made up—to use another term invented by Wojtyla—the *Srodowisko* (or single large network that embraced the various groups). The community expanded and, naturally, so did the span of topics covered. They talked about responsible parenthood as well as the role of women, which needed to be valued and respected more than it was. They talked about sexuality and the difficulties often encountered when trying to live it in a true dimension of love and reciprocity between man and woman: "They ought to learn how to be together a lot," Karol said, "before undertaking a more intimate relationship."

In Cracow, he made a second discovery, what he called "human love," "beautiful love." He realized very quickly that this vocation to love was the element of closest contact with the young people. So he maintained that young people had to be taught to love. "Love isn't something that one learns; and yet there is nothing that's so necessary to learn."

He argued—and this was surely a bold affirmation—that "the sexual instinct is a gift of God." Yet, he also continually reminded the young people that desire mustn't be separated from love. "Love means desiring the good of the other, offering oneself for the good of the other. When as the outcome of the gift of themselves for the good of another, a new life is born, that donation of self must flow from love."

As a priest, he certainly couldn't bracket the teaching of the Church. He judged that it was his duty to constantly recall those principles, without fear of seeming to be too demanding. Neither did he want to do nothing but moralize. And he wrote, signing himself *Wujek*, to a young woman from the group named Teresa:

> People imagine Wujek would like to see everybody married. But I think that this is a false image. [...] Authentic love leads us outside ourselves to affirm others: to dedicate ourselves to the cause of man, to the people and, above all, to God. Matrimony has meaning [...] if it gives the opportunity for a love of this sort, if it evokes the capacity and necessity to love this way, if it draws one out of the shell of individualism (of various sorts) and out of egocentrism. It's not enough to want to accept a love like this. One has to know how to give it, and often it's not ready to be received. Many times it's necessary to help it get formed.

For Karol Wojtyla, those years represented a formative moment in his personal maturation. It was those young people, those couples with their questions, with their doubts, and above all, with their experiences, who pointed the way for him to enter into an understanding of human reality. Hence, they were his first educators. They inspired not just his studies and the books that he would write, but his own pastoral and missionary disposition. Finally, they taught him the type of resistance to use against a dictatorship that claimed to have absolute dominion over persons and their consciences in order to reduce all of society to submission—and in this way to subject even the Church.

That was something of which Archbishop Stefan Wyszynski, the new archbishop of Gniezno and Warsaw, would have a bitter taste. He was a great personality, an expert in social and economic questions, combative, and loyal to his fatherland. In the war years, he had worked in the underground and had incredibly escaped arrest by the Gestapo. With the death of Cardinal Hlond, Wyszynski was appointed primate of the Polish church at the age of only forty-seven. Though he knew the risks he was taking, he had immediately accepted the offer tendered by the regime to attempt a dialogue between Catholics and Marxists, at least within the compass of concrete situations.

Some voices hostile to the choice of Wyszynski were raised within the episcopate; and, even in Rome, a few people at the Vatican grimaced. Yet, Wyszynski charged ahead, hoping that in this way he could stop what he called the process of "spiritual hemorrhaging"; and he signed the "accord" of 1950. This agreement would commit the bishops not to block the action of the government in the economic and political sphere, while the government would safeguard the rights of the Church in the area of cultic practice, religious teaching, and charitable work. The immediate result was a lessening of the pressure on the Catholic community and civic society. However, it lasted only a few months.

News came from Rome that Pope Pius XII had refused to name residential bishops in the dioceses of the ex-German western and northern territories that had been assigned to Poland after the war. It was not an *a priori* refusal, but motivated exclusively by the lack of a political "systemization"—which had yet to be agreed upon between Germany and Poland—of the Oder-Neisse border.

The Warsaw government wasn't interested in reasons; or, even worse, it thought that the Holy See had no intention of recognizing the new borders of the Polish state. In any event, a violent antireligious campaign broke out: the government closed the minor seminaries; it confiscated thousands of acres belonging to the Church; it seized the *Caritas* organization; and it arrested many priests. It even struck the episcopate in the person of Monsignor Czeslaw Kaczmarek: the bishop of Kielce, after the usual farcical trial, was condemned to twelve years in prison.

During these same weeks, the persecution of believers was ratcheted up in all the other countries of central and eastern Europe. It was in Czechoslovakia that it undoubtedly reached the most tragic and devastating level.

The archbishop of Prague, Josef Beran, who had been in the Nazi concentration camps of Terezìn and Dachau, was put under house arrest and then interned. There followed the unilateral breaking of diplomatic relations with the Holy See. On the night between the April 13 and April 14 of 1950, at the prompting of the Ministry of Internal Affairs, a gigantic roundup was organized on the scale of a military operation. The police invaded monasteries and deported all the religious.

In September, it was the turn of the Sisters and cloistered nuns. There were more arrests and more trials. Bishops were condemned to life imprisonment and disappeared into gulags.

The Church of Czechoslovakia was apparently destroyed, reduced to zero. Yet, who knows how it would manage to resist in the catacombs, and survive?

Chapter Nineteen

THE PROLETARIAT REBELS

I t was March 5, 1953; the announcement of Stalin's death shook the communist world like an earthquake. There was general mourning, especially in the more dogmatic and ideological "bases," and there was also some genuine and deep sorrow. It is equally true, though, that many people were weeping crocodile tears, while heaving sighs of relief.

Ever since the time, some five years before, when the regimes of "popular democracy" had been set up in eastern Europe, the Soviet empire had been dominated by the Great Terror. The machine of repression had produced an endless chain of deaths, imprisonments, and deportations. It had crushed not only its opponents, but also orthodox militants, even leaders like Janos Kadar in Hungary or Gustav Husak in Czechoslovakia.

Then there was the group who, under the guidance of Malenkov, had taken over from Stalin: it was concerned, above all, with putting an end to the massacres. They indicted the head of the security services, Lavrenti Beria, had him arrested and then executed. They adopted a series of "liberal measures," including an amnesty; and invited their "brother" parties to set up a collective management and to make concessions to their populations. Only in Poland did this turnaround, mostly cosmetic as it was, create serious problems.

In the months before, the Polish government had been repeatedly called to order by Moscow, which forced it to speed up the pace of Sovietization. After subjugating civil society, it had begun to make frontal attacks on the Church. First, it issued the most severe kind of administrative sanctions. Then a new constitution, though it ratified the separation of church and state, had actually subordinated one to the other. Finally, that incredible decree came out, enabling the government to appoint and dismiss parish priests and bishops, as well as oversee every juridical act concerning the Church and, furthermore, requiring all the clergy to swear a loyalty oath to the people's republic.

This was an abnormal, unconstitutional initiative. Yet many people thought the government was deliberately making a show of strength to force the bishops to adopt a more submissive attitude. Then—it was thought—the two parties would get together around the table and come to reach some compromise or other. Of course, it was only to be expected that in the future, the Church would have less say and less space in civil society.

In those very days, the news came of the death of the "little father of the peoples." The Polish leaders—all of them Stalinists, beginning with the party secretary, Boleslaw Bierut—suddenly found themselves orphaned, without their all-powerful protector who had supported them against their internal opposition. Feeling themselves to be in danger, they thought they could make themselves look good in the eyes of their new bosses in the Kremlin by taking even harsher repressive measures.

Thus, although Stalin had disappeared, Stalinism, at least in Poland, remained. Instead, paradoxically, the antireligious campaign grew much more intense after the death of the dictator.

The bishops, moreover, could not keep silent. The decree on appointments, if carried out, would have jeopardized the very survival of the Church. Wyszynski intervened. Then, more or less underlining the same arguments as the primate's, the

bishops conference issued a joint declaration: "It is not permit-
ted—it is written—to place what is of God on the altar of Cae-
sar. *Non possumus*!"

The reaction from the regime was immediate and unpre-
cedentedly brutal. Eight bishops wound up in prison, as did a
thousand priests, religious, and nuns. Two priests were condemned to death; although the sentence was fortunately com-
muted to life imprisonment. The weekly *Tygodnik Powszechny*
had to close because it was "guilty" of refusing to publish a
funeral eulogy of Stalin. Religious instruction was eliminated
from the schools. The faculties of theology in the universities
were eliminated, and the taxes on religious property were raised.

More repressive actions were yet to come. On the nights of
the September 25 and September 26, 1953, a number of government emissaries appeared at the episcopal palace of Warsaw
to arrest Cardinal Wyszynski, "I don't see the legal basis of this
decision," the primate objected. To emphasize the arbitrariness
of the proceedings he took nothing with him but his breviary
and rosary. After various transfers, he was taken to Komancza,
to a monastery on the eastern frontier. He would stay there in
confinement for thirty-seven months. Like him, the Polish
church, although formally free, was in confinement.

Wojtyla, to an infinitely lesser extent, was also caught up in
those repressive provisions. He had recently become an assistant to the chair for Christian ethics at the Jagellonian University; now he found himself jobless after the forced closing of the
faculty of theology.

Two years before this, his life had undergone another decisive change. The man whom he considered a second father,
Cardinal Sapieha, had died. The archdiocese of Cracow had
been entrusted to Eugeniusz Baziak, but only provisionally. Since
it could not impose its own candidate, the regime had not accepted the appointment made by the Vatican.

Archbishop Baziak, however, carried out all functions and
had the authority of an archbishop. Thus, picking up an old

project of Sapieha's, he let Wojtyla know that it would be better for him to dedicate himself to scholarly work. Then—but this time his tone was peremptory—he asked him to prepare to take the qualifying examination as a university lecturer. Karol had tried to resist. He didn't want to abandon the parish of Saint Florian and the groups that he had been looking after for some time now, the young people, the university students, the couples. In the end, after obtaining permission to keep up the pastoral contacts, he had accepted and began to prepare, even though it went against the grain.

For his thesis, he had thought of doing a monograph on the ethics of German philosopher Max Scheler (1874–1928). He developed such a passion for the subject that he managed not only to work out his own mature philosophical identity, but also to find a point of encounter and a synthesis between two currents of thought: the philosophy of being, that is, Thomism, which he had studied in the Angelicum at Rome, and the philosophy of consciousness, that is, phenomenology, which he had learned more recently through Edmund Husserl and, of course, Scheler.

To put it rather schematically, Karol grafted the phenomenological method to his earlier Aristotelian-Scholastic formation, which was more bound up with objectivity, hence more attentive to general problems and to the principles of cosmology. He believed that phenomenology was better adapted to grasp and express subjectivity, addressing the questions about consciousness and human freedom, as well as moral choices. In this way, Karol had, on the one hand, avoided the risks of subjectivism and individualism; and, on the other hand, he had succeeded in marking out a path of research that moved from human reality, from lived experience, to arrive at the theoretical-moral plane of metaphysics. At the center, as the unifying element, was the human person, or rather, every single person, unique and unreplicable in all the universe.

In the philosophy of Wojtyla, and especially in his most

important work, *Person and Act*—a book that even then bore his own unmistakable stamp—there was a new understanding of humans, as the bearers of a moral truth, hence the trustees of their own responsibility, their own freedom. At the same time, there was an interpretation of the historical moment headed in a direction diametrically opposed to that of the totalitarianism then reigning: a totalitarianism that by taking away from people their power of choice and self-determination was stripping them of their native dignity as persons.

With the faculty of theology in Cracow closed, Karol went to teach ethics in Lublin, at the only church-run university in the communist world. There, in that somewhat protected oasis, he could compare his reflections with those of a group of professors who were quite young and who also had some very innovative ideas. These professors were resolved to fight the great politicalphilosophical battle with Marxism on its own turf, that of the liberation of the human person, but starting out from a humanism that had room in it for the individual, for the essence of humanity.

Meanwhile, after only three years, a second jolting announcement had thundered down on the communist world. The Twentieth Congress of the Soviet communist party had already closed up shop. At the last moment, the delegates were informed that there would an extraordinary, closed-door session; even foreign delegations would be barred. On the morning of February 25, 1956, amid absolute silence, and in the face of an incredulous, stunned audience, Nikita Khrushchev fired point-blank at Stalinism, at the "cult of the personality" that Stalin had introduced, and at the horrifying crimes with which Stalin had stained his hands.

The new czar was himself implicated—as were all the new leaders—in those misdeeds. For that very reason, Krushchev had ordered the destruction of certain documents in the archives to prevent their contents from becoming known. To distance himself more sharply from his predecessor, he had decided to deliver the indictment in person, liquidating thirty years of gulags, deportations, and mass assassinations. They were condemned as "degenerations," not of Bolshevism, but of those who had been in charge.

Everyone was traumatized, even in the West, especially after the text of the "secret report" appeared on June 4 in *The New York Times*. First and foremost, however, it was obviously a tremendous blow on the other side of the iron curtain. Bierut, the Polish leader, was emotionally overwhelmed; he had a heart attack in Moscow and died a few days later. When the news arrived in Poland, it was like pouring gasoline on the fire of popular protests already in progress against the salary-freeze and the shortages of food and housing.

In Poznan, the largest industrial center in the country, the workers went on strike. The march, almost certainly led by revisionist groups, quickly turned into an anti-Soviet demonstration. The headquarters of POUP was trashed, stores were looted, and the prison was attacked. Caught off guard and frightened, the government lost its head and reacted by sending in the tanks. The result was a bloodbath, with seventy-four killed and five hundred injured. There were arrests, trials, and sentences.

Four months passed, and the consequences of the revolt were clear to see. Wladislaw Gomulka, the greatest exponent of the "Polish way to communism" was triumphantly elected first secretary of the party.

Khrushchev plummeted down on Warsaw in a rage, convinced that the Poles were trying to unhinge the socialist system; he already had half a mind to call in the Red Army. Gomulka managed to handle him, persuading this Russian that there was no danger; and he was given a free hand. The Russian advisors were sent home. The government prepared a vast plan of reforms and liberalizing measures. Above all, it changed its attitude toward the Catholic Church. Wyszynski was set free; the other bishops were released from prison; and the decree about church appointments was modified. In this way, the Church's autonomy was recognized and, once again, it could savor its freedom; civil society benefitted too.

Nevertheless, the freedom granted was a closely monitored sort; it didn't last very long. Still, what had happened at Poznan, with all its limitations, and even though it never went beyond the "internal" logic of communism, constituted a historic event. For the first time the proletariat had challenged the regime, which was supposed to represent the working class and support its claims. To press the point further, beyond the political and ideological labels, it must be said quite simply that those men had revolted against a power that wished to deprive them of their dignity as human beings.

These were the very same conclusions that Wojtyla himself was reaching. As a matter of fact, his concern for the human person had never arisen—as he would recall years later—in opposition to Marxism. His conception of the person and his vision of history had not been formed "against" anyone or anything. It had taken its inspiration from the Gospel and from a humanism in which the person, respected in his or her fundamental rights, has primacy over things, over technology, ideologies, and socio-economic systems.

In the real world, unfortunately, events were still going in a very different direction. The Hungarian uprising had broken out. Khrushchev, the same man who shortly before had set "de-Stalinization" in motion, and who had been acclaimed for this all over the West, this same man personally gave the order to crush the revolt with tanks.

Cardinal Mindszenty had been set free by the insurgents and was on his way to Parliament to launch an appeal for reconciliation and unity in the struggle against the occupiers. Suddenly the cardinal found himself facing Soviet armored vehicles in the streets of Budapest. He was forced to take refuge in the American embassy, where he would remain for fifteen years. The "thaw" within the empire had ended before it even began.

Chapter Twenty

"A SLAVIC POPE IS COMING"

Karol was convinced that his life had now entered upon
its definitive path.
To be sure, he would have preferred being a different kind of priest, in a parish, in close contact with people's
concrete problems. He would have continued to teach and write
books. He would have kept his own pastoral space, maintaining his ties with academics, students, and families.

Then, one day in July, he received a telegram. Somehow
they had managed to track him down at the Masuri Lakes, where
he was canoeing with a group of friends. The telegram upset his
comfortable lifestyle and security. They wanted to make him a
bishop. He was asked to present himself immediately to Cardinal Wyszynski in Warsaw.

At that very moment, he didn't like this situation at all,
partly because he knew nothing about it. Or rather, he knew
only that he had been destined to have a university career, and
that his name had never been put on the list of episcopal candidates. What had happened?

What happened was that Monsignor Baziak had ignored
the list. Since he had to find a replacement for the auxiliary
bishop of Cracow, who had died a few months before, he had
chosen Karol—an intellectual, someone who was only thirty-

eight. The archbishop, to avoid interference, had sent his proposal directly to Pope Pius XII.

In some ways, Wyszynski had been bypassed, and this was
just one more reason why he wanted to get to know Wojtyla.
When he had him face to face, and asked him if he would accept the post, he was struck by the younger man's readiness. In
fact, Karol responded with another question: "Where do I sign?"
He signed, and only then did he ask: "Now can I go back to my
hike?" That is, he didn't want to leave his young people. The
cardinal consented with a smile.

He was ordained a bishop on September 28, 1956. In the
Wawel cathedral, one could see something like the whole history of the new bishop out on display. His theater colleagues
were there, along with the workers from Solvay, the families of
Niegowic, his first parish, and of Saint Florian. His professors
from the seminary and from Lublin came, along with the intellectuals and the academics who looked after the ordination service. At the culmination of the rite, as the *Te Deum* was intoned,
an old friend from the marble quarry, called him by his boy-
hood name, and cried out: "Lolek, don't let anyone bring you
down!"

So His Excellency, "Lolek," began his apprenticeship as a
bishop. One by one, he visited the parish churches of the area
assigned to him. He also continued to teach, traveling back and
forth between Cracow and Lublin. He continued to meet with
young people and new couples. Above all, he continued his
ministry in the confessional, which he wouldn't have given up
for anything in the world.

Karol drew upon that experience, and hence from his knowledge of the most varied matrimonial situations, of conjugal cri-
ses, but also of the most wonderful love stories, as starting points
for his scholarly and literary work. In an essay entitled, "Love
and Responsibility," he dealt with sexuality and with female
"frigidity," which he thought, in some cases, was a consequence
of male egoism. The man, he wrote, "while seeking his own

satisfaction, often in a brutal manner, does not know or wish to understand the subjective desires of the woman, nor the objective laws of the sexual process going on inside her."

Those were surely daring words for that time, and all the more so because they were written by a bishop. Just as daring was his view of married life contained in *The Jeweler's Shop*, a verse play that told the story of three different but interconnected couples. One need only read the beginning to grasp the intensity with which Karol had approached the great mystery of love.

The speaker here is Teresa, the protagonist of the first story:

Andrea has chosen me and asked for my hand. It happened this evening between five and six.... We were walking around the square on the right when Andrea turned and asked me: "Will you be my life companion?" He put it just like that. He didn't ask: "Will you be my wife but: my life companion."

Those were years of great novelty. Pius XII died; and the cardinals elected a seventy-seven-year-old pope, hence a transitional pope more or less as everyone thought. However, John XXIII called an ecumenical council, which would throw wide open the doors and windows in the Church, prompting a general renewal.

When the Vatican Council opened on October 11, 1962, Karol was there in that long procession of white miters that crossed Saint Peter's Square. He was no longer an auxiliary bishop, but the capitular vicar of Cracow. Monsignor Baziak had died of a heart attack. While waiting for a successor they had assigned Wojtyla to run the archdiocese on a provisional basis.

He returned home in December and found himself involved in yet another attack on the episcopacy. Once again, the government had taken up its struggle against religion. The building

of the Berlin Wall had divided Europe in two, and signaled the
beginning of the Cold War. Moscow had forced its satellite countries to return to the most rigid "orthodoxy."

The first to suffer the consequences of this was the Church,
especially the Church in Poland. Backed by strong financial re-
sources, the government unleashed a violent atheistic campaign
that was clearly designed to achieve the complete secularization
of society.

There was a new change at the summit of the Church Universal—the death of Pope John and the election of Paul VI—
but there were also new developments in the Polish church. At
the end of 1963, Karol learned he had been chosen as archbishop of Cracow. His cause had been promoted, to some extent, by the communist authorities themselves, who had crossed
out no fewer than six names proposed by Wyszynski. They had
rejected them because they were convinced they could find—in
that careful student of Marxism, Karol Wojtyla—an interlocutor who was more conciliatory and malleable than the cardinal
primate.

During this period, Karol had to follow the Council, so he
was often far from Cracow. That event was, for him, a great
education; it deepened his knowledge of doctrine and updated
his ideas about pastoral care. In the first session, he simply listened; but later he became an active participant. He made important speeches on religious freedom and atheism. He was called on
to collaborate in the drafting of *Gaudium et Spes*, which revo-
lutionized the Church's position on the contemporary world.

As Vatican II drew to a close, an extremely serious crisis
broke out within the Warsaw government. Its source was an
initiative that, in the spirit of the Council, grew out of the process of "purification of memory" that had led to the acknowledgment of the sins committed by Christians down through the
ages. The Polish bishops, taking this same new attitude of the
Church as their point of departure, had sent a letter to the German bishops, with the goal of promoting reconciliation between

their two peoples. The letter ended with the sentence: "We stretch out our hands forgiving you and asking you to forgive us."

They were told they never should have done it. They were accused of treason, of political interference, and even of having "absolved" the Nazi criminals. Wojtyla was personally attacked in a public letter that the Solvay workers were made to sign. Wyszysnki had his passport taken away. And the government set out to systematically boycott the 1966 celebrations of the Millennium, commemorating the anniversary of Poland's baptism and the foundation of the national state.

The statue of the "Black Madonna" was actually "kidnaped" as it was being carried on pilgrimage around the country. A visit by Pope Paul VI was blocked, and the borders were shut down for more than a month during the culminating phase of the ceremonies.

All of this was part of the new political climate, that is, the so-called "restoration," started by Brezhnev, the czar who had been installed in the Kremlin. The strategy of the Polish government was equally evident, as it sought to show that the Church no longer had the influence upon society that it once had. However, this effort turned into a resounding failure. The Millennium celebrations were an extraordinary success, primarily on the religious and spiritual levels. The regime discovered it had totally miscalculated Wojtyla and even more concerning the prospect of his representing an "alternative" to Wyszynski.

Meanwhile, Karol had become a cardinal. Free now from other tasks, he could finally play the role of archbishop on a full-time basis. His visits to the parishes went on for weeks: he administered confirmation, went to comfort the sick in home visits, and presided over couples' renewing their marriage vows. And he never skipped his meetings with young people. They were drawn by the image of the Church that Karol brought to them from the Council and personally embodied—a Church whose face was now predominantly communitarian, charismatic, and lay, rather than hierarchical, institutional, and clerical.

In the meantime, relations with the authorities were getting increasingly difficult. There had been trouble already over the issue of building churches in new districts, which had provoked—as it did in the industrial center of Nova Huta—bloody clashes between Catholics and the forces of law and order. Police hunts for youth groups now intensified, and a whole series of restrictions crippled pastoral work in the universities. The archbishop was repeatedly forced to intervene; but he did so in the name of human rights and individual and collective freedoms. He never stooped to the level of ideology, as his adversaries hoped he would, so that they could counterattack.

The years passed, with popular insurrections regularly breaking out—the "little revolutions," as Cardinal Wyszynski called them: because, while they confirmed the gradual failure of Marxism, and of "real socialism," in its Polish version, these "revolutions" were never followed by real changes in direction.

After the Poznan revolt, 1968 saw the protest by the students and intelligentsia. The government—inventing a Zionist peril in a country where there were practically no more Jews—took advantage of the situation to liquidate the revisionists and encourage a wave of nationalism. People like philosopher and Marxist scholar Lezek Kolakowski chose the path of exile.

And in that same time period in Czechoslovakia, Soviet tanks stifled the Prague "springtime." Alexander Dubchek's dream of "socialism with a human face" had lasted only eight months. Hopes of reforming communism ended there, forever.

In 1970, in the port-city of Gdansk on the Baltic, the workers rose in revolt, and orders to stop the protest arrived at once. The terrible "special units" of the militia had already gone into action, but the government went further and called in the army. There was a massacre. The dead were hastily buried, and their families were warned not to sue. Everything had to be covered up. But the Kremlin wasn't satisfied. The Soviets sacked Gomulka and replaced him with Edward Gierek, a highly pragmatic manager. He opened up to the West, but left the party in the hands of a generation of opportunists in their forties, cynical and corrupt.

The crucial year of 1976 arrived. In March, Wojtyla was called to the Vatican to preach the *Spiritual Exercises* for Lent; there he had a worldwide platform, from which he could denounce the spread of the kind of case-hardened atheism that systematically violates the rights of believers. In June, Poland saw the usual pattern of a sudden rise in prices and a popular revolt that was quickly put down. This time, though, the students and intellectuals stood side by side with the workers. Polish society rediscovered its own strength, its own subjectivity, binding together the strands of a fruitful solidarity (*solidarnosc*) that would go far.

The Church served as the glue and protective support for this union. Putting aside an attitude of mere denominational confrontation, of sole antagonist of the regime, the Church became a safeguard for all the social forces, as it defended national identity and civil rights. Wojtyla represented the cutting edge of this Church. He protected workers, intellectuals, students, Jews, revisionists, and dissidents.

When Wyszynski, who had now turned seventy-five, sent in his resignation, the Polish leaders officially asked the Vatican if he could stay on at his post. That way they thought they could stop Wojtyla from becoming primate; but they failed to block the move. In the spring of 1978, the archbishop of Cracow was like a river in flood. He gave dozens of speeches and homilies to unmask the chronic ineptitude of a regime that knew nothing but methods of repression and censure, but also a message to uplift and sustain the new Poland that was coming to birth, the Poland of the young, the Poland that had recovered the meaning of its own history.

Then came October 16. Two popes had died, Pope Paul VI, and a few weeks later Pope Luciani, John Paul I. A second conclave was needed. The incredible happened. As a great Polish poet, Juliusz Slowacki, had "foreseen" more than a century before:

Amidst all the discord,
God sets an immense bell ringing,
He opens the throne to a Slavic Pope....
Much energy is needed to rebuild the Lord's world;
and that is why a Slavic Pope is coming,
a brother of the peoples....